Sarah Sands is a former newspaper editor and former editor of BBC Radio 4s Today programme. She has published books about mythology, monasteries, nature and faith.

In memory of my brother, Kit Hesketh Harvey, and dedicated to all those who loved him.

Sarah Sands

CONSTELLATIONS AND CONSOLATIONS

AUSTIN MACAULEY PUBLISHERS™

LONDON * CAMBRIDGE * NEW YORK * SHARJAH

A CIP catalogue record for this title is available from the British Library.

ISBN 9781035865802 (Paperback)
ISBN 9781035865819 (ePub e-book)
ISBN 9781035865826 (Audiobook)

www.austinmacauley.com

First Published 2024
Austin Macauley Publishers Ltd®
1 Canada Square
Canary Wharf
London
E14 5AA

I would like to express admiration to the new Hansa for their peace building mission along historical trade routes.

And my love and gratitude to my darling husband, Kim.

Table of Contents

Preface   11

Contents   19

Chapter 1: Perpetual Light   22

Chapter 2: Cathedrals and Choristers   45

Chapter 3: The Hanseatic Connection   60

Chapter 4: Baltic Journey   93

Chapter 5: Requiems   117

Chapter 6: Words and Psalms   142

Chapter 7: A Note from Kit's Lake Ely   149

Chapter 8: Constellations and Consolations   164

Preface

This world is but a thoroughfare of woe and we are pilgrims passing to and fro.

—The Knight's Tale, The Canterbury Tales

In Thomas Mann's masterpiece novel about sickness, *The Magic Mountain*, the narrator identifies two images of death. "In one aspect, death was a holy, a pensive, a spiritual state, possessed of a certain mournful beauty. In another, it was quite different. It was precisely the opposite; it was very physical, it was material, it could not possibly be called either holy, or pensive, or beautiful—not even mournful."

When I read this passage, I was in the headlights of a very physical aspect of death. My beloved elder brother, Kit, had not been answering his phone for a few days. My text messages went from fondly exasperated, 'Why aren't you answering?', 'Where are you?' to some cross checks. It was when his musical partner, James McConnel, said that Kit had not shown up to rehearsal that cold dread set in.

A friend from the village went to check the vestry of the church where Kit had been living after a wretched divorce. The wife of the villager phoned me, barely able to speak.

I asked in a faraway voice, not my own, if Kit had hung himself. Then I went to the police station and onto the church where two young police constables stood behind a cordon and advised me not to go in. "It is not how you would want to remember him."

In fact, Kit died from natural causes, an exhausted heart, that just gave out. He was in the bath, listening to radio 3, and that is where he was found two days later. The coroner noted that the blood supply to his heart was reduced to less than 20 per cent, and yet he had just completed a season of pantomime, was writing a radio 4 drama, had almost finished an opera libretto, was performing cabaret and, days earlier had written an anthem for a processional cross, to music by Roderick Williams and to be presided over by the former Archbishop of Canterbury, Rowan Williams, at Magdalene College, Cambridge.

The coroner's report was all the more disturbing in this regard. It recorded in its internal examination that 'the brain was severely autolysed and reduced to a structureless, pale, semi-liquid mass weighing approximately 1130g'.

How could it be that a mind as curious and creative as my brother's, so hard at work, could three days later be nothing more than a semi-liquid mass. Was death so reductive, so utilitarian?

And yet, something of Kit's spirit could not be quenched. A fortnight after he died I went with Kit's son, Rollo, and my son, Henry, to watch Rowan Williams take the service for the inaugural performance of the *Vision of the Cross* anthem for the Cross of the Cosmos. The delicate, burnished silver cross with its blue enamel centre on which was drawn the lamb of God moved slowly up the nave, and those at the side stalls would have seen the words engraved: 'Thy Will Be Done.'

The music was mysterious and uplifting. One refrain from the anthem rang out: "Where science cannot grant us sight/illumed by a greater light. Dust may be reordered/Dust we may restore."

A couple of weeks before Kit died, Henry's dad, my former husband, Julian, had gone missing on a hike on Mount Baldy in California. As with Kit, it seemed unbelievable and then inevitable. Henry caught the first flight out to California to join a search, accompanied by an experienced climber who could predict the decisions Julian would have taken as a storm set in.

I watched on a live site the progress of this rescue team along a moving black line and a pin location. They stopped at the base cabin, where they hoped Julian might be sheltering. Then the line snaked slowly upwards and onwards further past trees and gullies through fresh six feet snowfalls.

Henry and the search party, which came eventually to include hundreds of volunteers, were up against freak snow fall, the heaviest for forty years, and were thwarted while there might have been hope. The language changed from rescue to recovery. Henry went back on a second search but Julian's body was eventually found by a hiker in June. He had been sitting, wrapped in a blanket, his phone beside him.

When Julian first went missing, my brother wrote an email message speculating about the 'unendurable image of that extraordinary flame, gradually freezing into extinction.'

That turned out to be what happened.

The service for Cross of the Cosmos came at a time when our private world seemed to have lost its axis. Rowan Williams took the metaphor of the Cross of the Cosmos to reflect on disorder and order. He has written poetry on the theme and particularly studied Bach and his harmony of the spheres. He had written of Augustine that, 'it is love that draws us back to our proper place, that pulls us back to stability and harmony.'

The two images that I had, of Kit's brain dissolving in water, and of Julian searching for a path in a mountain white out, both cried out for the balm of ritual, the restoration of peace and quiet. I seem to remember murmuring the words peace, grace and mercy as a kind of private chant.

Kit and Julian were the same age and had worked together. Kit wrote the screenplay for *Maurice*, the Merchant Ivory film which was the follow up to the success of *Room with a View*, which is the film for which Julian will be most remembered. It was a clip from this film which was played during the In Memoriam section at the Oscar ceremony in 2024. Julian's voice sounded so youthful, hopeful, English.

Julian was supposed to star in *Maurice* but bolted just before the start of filming. He wandered across the world until finally a storm stopped him in his tracks.

Julian and Kit also shared a faith, differently expressed.

Julian had a theatrical feel for religion, particularly the Stations of the Cross procession at Easter, which I remember him leading at our local church in London at the height of his fame in his early twenties. The congregation looked curiously at this blazing figure, with blond locks and actorly poses.

For Kit, his faith was founded on his upbringing as head chorister at Canterbury Cathedral, a training in practice and discipline and moments of the sublime. He went on to study under John Rutter as a music scholar at Cambridge.

For Kit's funeral, I had an idea of borrowing the Cross of the Cosmos but family members were reticent about holding it. It felt quite a statement and there were insurance implications. Julian would have relished carrying it. I reckon that both Julian and Kit recognised the figure of death, unflinchingly.

In his last year, Kit struck up a musical friendship with Henry's wife, Anna, who had recently joined a choir of sacred music, called Cambridge Voices. Anna's mother is from Estonia, a musical nation, and she went on to study here at the Royal College of Music.

Kit and Anna chattered about Tallis and Byrd and Rutter. While Henry was searching for Julian in California, driven by determination and imagination of Julian battling the storm, I stayed with Anna for company and to help out with their son, our grandson, Billy. I babysat along with my daughter Tilly while Anna drove to Cambridge for a rehearsal of Cambridge Voices. She was reluctant to go but I said that music of the spheres would be an antidote to fear and limbo.

When Kit was found dead ten days later, Anna immediately knew which music we should have at the funeral. Kit would have wanted Tallis's *O Nata Lux* Sir John Rutter's *A Gaelic Blessing* and Charles Wesley. Grace, mercy, peace. And the coffin was carried out of the church to Kit's recording of his own defiant ballad: *I was Cabaret*. The musical director of the funeral was Kit's dear friend and musical partner, James McConnel.

I chose to read for the funeral Elizabeth Bishop's *I Am In Need of Music*, which again expressed to me a yearning for peace and stillness after the rupture of bereavement. It seemed to me that music, and above all sacred music, was the promised light and the trumpet call that waited beyond death. The Image of water, of rivers as paths, also felt religious.

A few months after Kit died, I went to see Sir John Rutter, his old tutor. He had come to Kit's funeral and written a charming note that he was pleased that we had chosen his anthem *A Gaelic Blessing* for the procession of the coffin and that Kit would have professionally appreciated that its brevity meant that pallbearers needed to pick up the pace. They had just under two minutes to reach the altar.

These things had to be got right. Sir John Rutter told me that he could always tell who had been a cathedral chorister because of their perfectionism. A picture hung slightly askew would cause a shadow of pain.

Kit's vestry may have been shabby and plain but it was extraordinarily neat, his pairs of shoes exactly aligned in rows on the stairs, to his raised floor bedroom, his lyrics contained in carefully chosen moleskin notebooks which he always carried with him.

Former choristers might go to tremendous trouble on details that the rest of us would not bother about.

When Kit stayed with me, during his divorce, he had no money for a present, so he pressed the weed in our pond, made it into paper and wrote me a thank you letter. He wrote another poetic note to a younger male architect of whom he had grown fond: "With love, sunshine, care, drawn on blanketweed. Dare hymn the lilies."

It would have taken him at least a day, which he should have been spending on legal administration. Who can blame him?

He had beautiful Sanskrit style handwriting, and he used ink. I also understood from John Rutter the centrality of cathedrals in Kit's creative thinking. Kit's children went to schools in Ely and Norwich, and he would take his son Rollo by boat up the river to Ely from their home an hour away in order to make it more magical for him.

He had a project on the go, conserving wildlife at a former quarry lake in Ely. After he died, I went to look at the lake and there it was, in direct sight of Ely Cathedral. Of course, that is why he was drawn to it. He belonged there.

The other project that occupied him in his final months was working out a pilgrim route across Norfolk which would take in neglected churches which could do with the footfall. He was pretty broke by the time he died and had lost the home he built and loved in Cornwall, but he had come round to a kind of pilgrim life.

He was fond of his battered old transit van, which he particularly liked to park outside Highclere Castle, to the delight of his hostess and friend the Countess of Carnarvon. When I suggested that he traded it in for an actual car, he looked at me wistfully: " But it is like a magic carpet."

It is said that we are all characters from Chaucer's Canterbury Tales. I reckon Kit was the Host, the master of ceremonies, judge of the story telling, merry, witty and outward looking. I can hear the indignation of the master of words in the Host's dismissal of Sir Topaz's tale: " My God, put plainly in a word, Your dreary rhyming isn't worth a turd." Kit would also have known the route to Canterbury.

One excuse that I have for not taking a closer interest in Kit's failing heart, was that he never mentioned his health; he regarded it as a boring imposition on others. One of his later satirical songs was of a shy figure who found a way to shine to parties by listing all their allergies.

He became listless about possessions just when the divorce inventory was requested. He loved his piano and a Rupert Brooke war medal. I saved from the vestry a brass cross belonging to our grandfather, a script that he was writing with Julian, a trampled painting Kit had drawn of a swan on the lake at Ely, and a piece of prose he had earlier offered to me about his life as a cathedral chorister, which I shall reprint in this book.

We had both become animated by the pilgrim routes and their connection to the Hanseatic League, a medieval trading route which linked Norfolk to the Baltic states and finally to Russia. It laid the foundations for the European Union, although a more Northern, Lutheran temperament, and it bequeathed cathedrals in every Hanseatic city.

During this time, I became a trustee of the British Council, which seeks peace and prosperity through cultural relations. I came to recognise the Baltic states as an important new geopolitical alliance and as a route to peaceful democracies.

Kit's daughter, Gus, was living in King's Lynn, a Hanseatic trading post.

On a blazing summer day in late May 2023, we first visited Kit's lake at Ely, jumping into the water after a picnic of bread, cheese, and martini shots in thimbles provided by Emma Bridgewater, the pottery manufacturer, social reformer, pilgrim, and steadfast friend to Kit. Then we drove to Kit's church at Stoke Ferry where we said pilgrim prayers and played the choral music of his favourite composers, Charles Villiers Stanford and Mendelssohn. Kit's piano was there in the otherwise empty nave, a memory of his composition and also that the church had been the scene of gaiety as well as a contemplation, in particular high spirited reeling at his New Year's Eve parties.

The following day, we went on a pilgrimage to King's Lynn, where the medieval anchorite Julian of Norwich had visited the mystic Margery Kempe, and we sat down to a Hanseatic feast at the home of the historians Simon Thurley and Anna Keay. Henry had found at Kit's vestry his drawing of a pilgrim route through Norfolk which would take in local neglected churches and he embellished it. Kit's route now included the Indian restaurant in Swaffham and Kit's transit van repair shop. I like the realism of it and Kit would have laughed. He was both spiritual and satirical, ascetic and pagan.

Later in the summer, after a second search by Henry and rescue teams and helicopters on Mt Baldy, Julian's body was found.

I listened to the news of it on BBC Radio 4's Today, 1 July, knowing that its journalists would be sensitive to the fact that I used to edit this programme. The presenter, Mishal Husain, was pitch perfect, empathetic but professional as she announced that in tribute to Julian, the programme would play out to *O mio babbino caro*, Puccini, the music from *Room with a View*.

I stood absolutely still listening, as another younger self heard the music while holding a guide book to Florence, heavily pregnant and happy, waiting for Julian to finish filming.

We are multiple selves during our lifetimes which I had assumed to be cumulative but this time, it felt like a moment of quantum physics, as if time itself had broken down and in another world, I still existed as that young mother to be planning a different life. Music cuts through time.

Music for Julian, music always for Kit.

Later that month, I went to the Foreign Office to meet the then foreign secretary, James Cleverly, on British Council business.

I noted the painting on the wall in the room in which I was waiting. It was of St Cecilia, by the Viennese artist Edouard Veith. St Cecilia was martyred for her beheading after pledging her virginity to God on her wedding day.

She was inspired by hearing instruments at her wedding and singing 'in her heart only to God'. In 1584, she was made the patroness of church music.

Kit sang Benjamin Britten's Hymn to St Cecilia in Venice in 1977 with the Clare College choir in a concert with Monteverdi's Il Combattimento di Tancredi e Clorinda, arranged by the British Council.

I did not remark on this to James Cleverly, but would have raised it with the shadow foreign secretary, David Lammy, because I knew he would appreciate it. Lammy was a former chorister at Peterborough Cathedral. There is no such thing as an ex-chorister.

The foreign secretary was leaving shortly for Lithuania for a NATO summit which marked the accession of Sweden and the more painful progress of Ukraine. I had become increasingly interested in the Baltic axis, for its Hanseatic routes, its courage in the face of aggression, and for its music.

John Rutter said to me that if the choral tradition was waning in Britain, it was shining in Estonia. Imagine a country that rose up against Russia in 1989 by joining hands and singing. The choral revolution.

This book is an attempt to find a route through sadness to a mournful beauty. For me, it was a physical one, along the old Hanseatic route, and through sacred or contemplative music. Asked a fortnight before he died how he would like to be reincarnated, Ralph Vaughan Williams replied:

"Music, music. But in the next world, I shan't be doing music, with all the strivings and disappointments, I shall be being it."

Contents

Chapter 1

Perpetual Light: How I have come to appreciate the meaning of sacred music, the bridge between life and death, and the relationship between music and faith.

Chapter 2

Cathedrals and Choristers: The role of cathedrals in Kit's life and now mine, talking to fellow choristers including Kit's contemporary, Harry Christophers, who founded a sacred music singing group, The Sixteen. Kit began his life as a chorister at Canterbury Cathedral and looked for peace near his end at a lake in sight of Ely Cathedral, which was also the start of his drawn pilgrim route. The relationship between cathedrals and the Hanseatic trade route, anticipating the glories of Lubeck, Torun and Visby.

Chapter 3

The Hanseatic Connection: Finding out about the great trade route across the North Sea and the Baltic, which was also the route of Luther and choral music. Weaving in music as the answer to death and to war: The German centric Hanseatic route, precursor to the European Union, produced the conditions for Bach, Brahms and Beethoven and the Scandinavian dominance in classical music today.

Sibelius, Mahler and Arvo Part, music of freedom and defiance against military occupation. The choral revolution of the Baltic states against Soviet occupation. Visits to the Hanseatic heartlands of Lubeck and Visby.

Chapter 4

Baltic Journey: I begin my geographical journey, tracing the Hanseatic route from Copenhagen to Gdansk, Lithuania, Latvia, Estonia and Finland. I learn about the song festival crushed by the Soviets and revived again.

Chapter 5

Requiems: The Requiem is at the heart of the musical relationship with death. Kit wrote and James McConnel composed a requiem for Olaf Schmid, a Cornish chorister and a bomb disposal officer in the British Army, who was killed on his final tour in Afghanistan. The requiem was played at Kit's funeral and was finally staged on Armistice Day 2023. I trace the requiems of Mozart, Beethoven, Brahms and Britten and their relationships to personal sorrows and to war.

Chapter 6

Words and Psalms: Psalms are the texts for sorrow and joy, described as the 'poetry of exile'. They are meaningful for choristers, the composer Errollyn Wallen and John Rutter among others. They speak to tragic events in the Middle East, the Old Testament, the Jewish Lament, and darkness.

Chapter 7

A Note from Kit's Lake Ely: Kit enthused his beloved friend, Caroline Roboh, to purchase from Network Rail a former clay pit to revive nature and because of the view of Ely Cathedral. Kit put up a painstakingly aesthetic notice telling the public, in a small essay, that there were otters, kingfishers, nightingales, etc. there.

It is, however, mostly used by the public for parties and drugs.

But Caroline and I have sought guidance from nature experts including bird writer Stephen Moss, Jo Thomas from Wildfowl and Wetlands Trust, a quiet, devoted friend to Kit who had dedicated her life to the bittern and a Norfolk farmer and conservationist Ed Pope, who advised me to import buffalo. The chapter will chart the restoration of the lake and the colourful characters involved in the project.

Chapter 8

Constellations and Consolations: This chapter brings together the themes of the book. The Hanseatic theme culminates in the festival of Torun, Poland, with its Hanseatic parades and gigantic puppet of Copernicus, the pioneering scientist on the movements of the stars and planets. I then move across to the Shetlands which would be the far point of the UK Hanseatic route and where a space centre is being built by my friend.

And I write of Kit's final piece of work, the processional anthem for the Cross of the Cosmos, reminding us of the order of creation. This also takes us back to Bach and the music of the spheres. I end with plans for pilgrimages to the lake and music at the cathedral looking at the full moon over Ely. This is my vision for peace—consolations and constellations.

Playlist: For the audio version of the book.

- ❖ Wesley: Thou Wilt Keep Him in Perfect Peace.
- ❖ John Rutter: A Gaelic Blessing
- ❖ Stephen Sondheim: Being Alive
- ❖ Kit Hesketh, Harvey and James McConnel: Requiem Aeternam: From Olaf Schmid
- ❖ Kit and the Widow Glyndebourne
- ❖ Kit and the Widow No plumbers Left in Poland
- ❖ Kit and the Widow Norwegians on the Underground
- ❖ Sibelius: Finlandia
- ❖ Welsh choir: How Great Thou Art
- ❖ Kit and McConnel Swansong
- ❖ Kit and McConnel Lullaby
- ❖ Brahms German Requiem first movement
- ❖ Benjamin Britten War Requiem first movement
- ❖ Kit Hesketh, Harvey and James McConnel: I was Cabaret.

Chapter 1
Perpetual Light

Sacred Music: *The heart of things.*

Ye now have sorrow, but I will see you again and your heart will rejoice and your joy shall not be taken away.

—John 16.22

Applaud friends, the comedy is ended.

—Beethoven

I am in the stalls at Proms 69, during an unexpected heatwave in September 2023. Outside the Royal Albert Hall, life is flamboyantly al fresco. There are ball games and picnics in the park. A woman in a floral dress is flogging Mozart scores laid out on the grass, as if they are knocked off handbags. There is a humid, carnival atmosphere on the streets.

Inside the hall, we are watching scenes of the hereafter. The conductor, Raphael Pichon, and his choir and instrument ensemble are performing Mozart's Requiem in D Minor with some additional fragments of Mozart's sacred music, or complementary pieces.

Mozart was chronically ill and exhausted when he undertook the commission for a Requiem Mass in the winter of 1791. His unfinished Requiem was played at his funeral in December.

Of course, I look for evidence of his state of mind in his music, and think I can read it into it terror as well as consolation. I am being subjective because if we are in a state that is open to grief, we look for clues; music is universal and seems to come from beyond our universe.

The choir at the Proms is mighty, an expression of beautiful solemnity. The conductor then does something so simple it breaks all defences. A child, the chorister Malakai Bayoh, sings alone the anonymous Plainsong in Paradisum, a treble voice, an expression of purity, invoking the one who leads the dead souls to their rest.

In Paradisum deducant de Angeli:
In tuo adventu suscipant te Martyres,
Et perducant te in civitatem sanctum Jerusalem.
Chorus Angelorum te suscipiat,
Et cum Lazaro quondam paupere aeternam habeas requiem.

There is an English translation in the programme for those of us who do not know Latin, but there is an extra force in its original language. 'aeternam habeas requiem' is more lyrical than 'may you have eternal rest'.

A few weeks earlier, I had seen a group of pilgrims walking incongruously through a Saturday food market in Swaffham holding up a banner which read: "Latin Mass Society England and Wales."

I send a mocking iPhone pic of it on the family WhatsApp asking if anyone could think of a more niche cause. Now I see that it was an appeal not for breadth but for a deeper poetic meaning.

Sacred music, sung either in Latin or actually post Reformation German, goes to the heart of things. Reformation in Europe seemed less brutal than in Britain. Luther hung on to Latin chorales and even plain chant. Bach's music was true to this, even with his counterpoints.

In the desolation of bereavement, sacred music echoes from the ether. On news of death, RIP is hastily posted on X or Twitter. What do we mean by this?

Wishing eternal rest is a stunningly lovely thing to ask on behalf of someone, as I learned when death did not seem peaceful but full of anguish and regret.

In the same way, the language of the Psalms is patiently waiting to be understood when needed. Edmund de Waal, the brilliant potter and writer, calls the Psalms: 'the poetry of exile'. He is attracted by the Abrahamic faiths, as the son of a former Dean of Canterbury Cathedral brought up on medieval manuscripts, who traced his Jewish heritage to dispossessed Viennese. The exile may be of land or of spirit.

St Basil expressed the Psalms as an answering call to the longing; I experienced this in the period after Kit's death, the longing of the bereaved.

He wrote: "A psalm implies serenity of soul; it is the author of peace, which calms bewildering and seething thoughts. For it softens the wrath of the soul and what is unbridled it chastens. A psalm forms friendships, unites those separated, conciliates those at enmity. Who, indeed, can still consider him an enemy with whom he has uttered the same prayer to God? So that psalmody, bringing about choral singing, a bond, as it were, towards unity, and joining the people into a harmonious union of one choir, produces also the greatest of blessings, charity."

Harmony and charity are particularly hard qualities to retrieve in the throes of a death without longevity or final contentment. King Charles wrote a thoughtful letter to Kit's daughter, Augusta, about her father's particular quality of bringing happiness to others through music, wit, mischief and sweetness. He could do this even if he were full of despair. I and others missed much of his sorrows because he wore his troubles so lightly. He just gave and gave and gave until his heart burst.

But wrote the king, he was taken from us far too early. Choral singing can capture this heartache.

A father standing in the crowd of prommers lifts his daughter who is slightly too big to be carried but too small to see the stage. He wobbles under the burden of her slender form but she wraps her arms around her father's neck and cranes her own to see Malakai Bayoh. She is quite unself-consciously enjoying the boy's voice while I am in a haze of tears and heart strings.

It is still light when we leave the concert hall and the sound of traffic and party going voices has a quantum dimension to it. We must co-exist in multiple worlds. Also, the plain truth is that when someone dies, the rest of life goes on unheeding.

I am starting to see that sacred music, written explicitly for liturgy or with a more humanistic slant of Brahms, can deal with both sorrow and joy.

It is the intensity of the concurrent emotions which breaks and lifts the heart.

Two days before my brother's funeral, my younger son, Rafe, and his wife, Charlotte, had a baby girl. It was a playing out of the line from Shakespeare's *The Winter's Tale*: "Thou mettest with things dying, I with things newborn." Deepest sorrow and joy, all at once. I looked at the photograph of the glistening womb wrinkled baby on the chest of her mother, and her expression suffused with wonder, and thought of Kit sinking into the water at his journey's end.

In his book, *Song and Self: A Singer's Reflections on Music and Performance*, the British tenor Ian Bostridge describes music as, "the closest thing this side of revelation to a glimpse of the divine. Music helps us to deal with death, with its inevitability, its incomprehensibility, its necessity."

This would have been familiar to my brother as a head cathedral chorister because funerals were part of his duties from the age of eight. Canterbury Cathedral was his home, his world. I did not really appreciate this until on an early summer day, I went to see Sir John Rutter, who taught Kit at Clare College, Cambridge.

Sir John's home outside Cambridge is opposite the church; it has an emerald, tightly mown lawn and rose bushes leading to a river bank beyond which swans glide along the Ouse.

It is a setting of hard won tranquillity. His wife, Jo Anne, is absent, walking the pilgrim route to Camino de Santiago in Spain.

In the middle of the lawn is a fruit tree, planted in memory of their son, Christopher, who died aged nineteen, while crossing the road after choir practice. John Rutter's *Mass of the Children* was his profound response to the worst tragedy.

John Rutter describes himself as agnostic but music and faith share a foundation in mystery.

He asks: "Why does it bring tears to your eyes to hear a violin playing Bach? It is transcendental. I don't trust people who think their faith gives them simple answers it is wrong to make something complex simple."

Months later, I read an account by the journalist Dominic Lawson of the memorial service of his father, the former chancellor, Nigel Lawson. Despite Nigel Lawson's atheism, the address was given by the Archbishop of Canterbury, Justin Welby, and music included Bach's chorale, *Jesu Joy of Man's Desiring* and Mozart's *Laudamus Te* from the Great Mass in C Minor, sung by the soprano Kirsty Hopkins.

Lawson wrote: "I asked for this notoriously demanding aria, not just because of my father's life long devotion to Mozart, but also because it, incomparably, links grief with consolation of sublime beauty. If you do not have faith—and I, like my father, lack it absolutely—this is the best we can do."

Kit was a musician WITH faith but he was principally a cabaret performer, applauded for his verbal dexterity, his glittering disregard for boundaries, and his sense of the absurd. Stephen Fry said of him: "Kit could rhyme everything. Kit rhymed with wit and wit rhymed with Kit."

His career was to send up reverence for music from Sondheim fans to Glyndebourne.

His song about a pair of 'opera queens' on their way to Glyndebourne, in musical homage to Rossini was an early favourite.

Glyndebourne
You never listen
It's so easy
At Clapham common you bear to the right an
From there it's peasy
A straight line to Brighton
Well hello Sidcup and you bet I'm in a flap
(please
Just read the map
Jesus, I can do without this crap)
Alright, but never call me dozy bitch again
It's fifty minutes
We've been waiting
No more, I thought so
That's what's so
Frustrating
With the M 25
An hour, door to door
Leaves stacks of time to feed the cat
I know the road, but bugger that
You had to drive
We're off to Glyndebourne
To see a rather boring opera by Rossini
We both like Glyndebourne
It gives us scope to be particularly queeny
We never miss anything that they mount there
Save the electrification of thingy and that didn't count
We're off to Glyndebourne

To see a challenging and thoughtful barbiere
This year at Glyndebourne
They've got a Finnish bass who's big and blond and hairy
We couldn't rise
Quite to a private chop
Per
Still, but their eyes
When they see what I've got in my hamper'll go pop
I've done monkfish fenouil
In a wild redcurrant sauce
I drew blood for the brie
I've done tournedos of course
I dreamed of intermissions spent
With Bernard Haitink in a tent
Or sipping Puligny Montrachet beneath a perfect summer moon
I get a monoxidic splurge
Of what was souffle a l'asperge
And I get one heady hour of glorious Orpington in flaming June
Alright!
Not now!
Tais_toi!
Bald cow
What's that rattle?
Carburettor?
You said it's better
You said that you fixed it
We passed the last service station at Hickstead
Oh boy, this afternoon is turning out a riot
(Please
Will you be quiet
Please: I'll twist the big end while you try it)
Alright but don't ask me to fix it with my tights

We're off to Glyndebourne to fight the Philistines with all our merry comrades
Nowadays Glyndebourne
Is full of clients of pharmaceutical conglom'rates
They wouldn't know that it was Agnes Balt
Sa
Not if she sat on their faces and sang 'come scoglio' in alt
We had to mortgage half the flat, but got the stalls there
He knows the boy who did the costumes for the balls there
Ssh! Listen, what did she say
Would be following the news?
Live from Glyndebourne today
Yes she did!
Patricia Hughes!
No, I will not ask him the way
No, I refuse point blank, okay?
Because one can't, not in Bromley Central when one's wearing one's DJ
That woman's practically blind
D'you think she looks as if she'd find
The way to somewhere as frankly ludicrously recherche as glynde?
O Christ and there goes my champagne
I'm never doing this again
Dear God and now here comes the rain
I said we ought to take the train
Quickly let's just stick it
Over here
You got the ticket
Come on dear
Forget the proggy
Doorway B
Oh have it your way
Doorway C
Please excuse us

Stuck in town
Sulky git
Come on sit down
Phew!

But curiously what had struck John Rutter was Kit's spiritual seriousness, based on his training as a chorister.

He told me, to my surprise: "Being a chorister meant everything to Kit. I have known plenty of ex-choristers and the one thing I would say is that there no such thing as an ex-chorister."

It seemed very bleak to me that Kit ended his days living in the vestry, opposite his family home, with its blazing lights and cars coming and going. But there was a symmetry to it.

When my father died, a year earlier, Kit had insisted upon an all-night vigil at this church. The vigils probably came more naturally to him because he wrote at night, whereas I am an early riser.

One of my very many regrets I have was how impatient I was with Kit when he arrived slightly late for a 9.30 am vigil service we held for Julian in January 2023.

For that service, Anna, my daughter-in-law, played the wheezing organ at another little Norfolk church on the hill, and our breath was visible as the handful of us joined in, *Onward Christian Soldiers*.

Kit walked in half-way through and it was as if cymbals had awakened us. We thundered through the rest of the verses. A week later, Kit was dead.

I marvel that Kit's failing, exhausted heart had no effect on his lungs for his voice was strong until the end.

Shakespeare wrote, music has a dying fall, and contemplation of mortality is there within the great music. We listen to Beethoven or Bach and glimpse the end.

While our secular society pays little attention to death, and we prefer to spend money and attention on holidays rather than funerals, the dying notes of Beethoven's final works make it clear what he saw. And in times of war and national crisis, we can see it too. In the midst of life, we are in death.

What else is there, really? John Rutter notes wryly that the Sir Simon Rattle is not known as a conductor who loves tradition but for his 2022 Proms Concert, as the world staggered back from the Covid pandemic, he chose Vaughan

Williams' *Fifth Symphony*, written during the Second World War and based on the story of the *Pilgrim's Progress*.

Rutter says: "When the chips are down, you want the heavenly city of Jerusalem."

As the Psalms, it answered a longing for peace. The music critic Neville Cardus wrote: "The *Fifth Symphony* contains the most benedictory and consoling music of our time."

Many of the great choral works and hymns have come from those who have experienced war or personal tragedy.

Charles Hubert Parry, loved Germany and despaired of the outbreak of First World War. His hymn *Jerusalem*, composed in 1917, ends every Proms, and was particularly poignant in 2023 before the Israel Hamas war broke out once more.

And in extreme times, Simon Rattle and Ralph Vaughan Williams, the vicar's son, aligned.

In hindsight, Kit's death had a musical prescience. He had shed worldly possessions, finally asking only for his piano, which came from his musical heroes, Flanders and Swann, and stood in his empty church. The score above the open lid was his libretto from the *Bartered Bride*, about love.

He spent his last week drawing pilgrim routes and working on his anthem, the *Vision of the Cross*. He knew that the Requiem, created a decade ago by him for a fallen soldier, and recently set to music by his partner, James McConnel, was completed.

He did not know when his death would come and he was working harder than ever before, but there was also a kind of fading, I realise. He was asking for nothing and making no plans. He would have been feeling physically exhausted and I hope very much that what he experienced was the inner quieting of the storm that is at the heart of choral music.

My pilgrimage since Kit died has been geographical, spiritual and musical. I had none of Kit's musical training but I follow his trail in now listening almost entirely to radio 3. I have moved to heart over brain.

And I have listened with especial attention to the Proms in 2023.

This year that followed Vaughan Williams' *Fifth Symphony* we have had Cantatas, Choral Symphonies, Requiems. My evenings have resonated to Handel's *Samson* or Schumann's *Das Paradies und die Peri*. We have had Carl Philipp Emanuel Bach's *Heilig Ist Gott*, with a double choir, one for heaven one for earth. The expense of it! And when the chamber choir, BBC Singers, was targeted for cuts early in 2023, there was such an extravagant and unexpected public outcry that the BBC hurriedly retreated.

How can you explain the deep attachment to choral singing when it hardly features in everyday public life? The BBC learned the hard way what is expected from a public service broadcaster.

What has most moved me through this 2023 Proms season has been Beethoven, Mahler, and Sibelius. I have been thinking of Kit's meticulously drawn pilgrim routes and those medieval Hanseatic trade routes to Germany and across the Baltics. There seemed to be a high count of Finns at the Proms in 2023. They opened with a Finnish conductor, Dalia Stasevska, while Finnish Swedish mezzo soprano, Jenny Carlsted, sung in Mahler's *Third Symphony*.

Meanwhile, NATO naval exercises were taking place in the Gulf of Finland and troops in Estonia. War and peace. Life and death.

In times of war or catastrophe, personal or public, when the chips are down, you want the heavenly city of Jerusalem.

Sir Simon Rattle's last choice of music with the LSO at the Proms before departing Britain was Mahler's *Ninth Symphony*.

Herbert von Karajan described it as "music coming from another world, it is coming from eternity."

Mahler does not strictly count as sacred music but he wrote the music of death and beyond. His second Resurrection Symphony passes through an orchestral shriek of death to the choral peace of the afterlife.

His Ninth Symphony was written at the time of his diagnosis of heart disease and the last movement is regarded as a musical expression of the act of dying. Mahler does not flinch, setting to music the poems by German poet Friedrich Ruckert, written after the death of his daughter from scarlet fever.

You are a shadow by day
and a light by night;
You live in my lamentation
and do not die in my heart.

In 1907, four years after the setting of these poems, Mahler's own daughter, Anna Maria, also died of scarlet fever. Mahler told his friend, Guido Adler, that he could not have written those songs after his daughter had died, it would have been too painful to bear.

Mahler died in 1911, at the age of fifty, and was buried in his daughter's grave.

Mahler's *Ninth*, inspires solemn awe. Rutter says that we need different answers and therefore, must ask different kinds of questions when confronting life and death. He says 'Is it true?' is the wrong question.

Augustine puts it this way: "it is not the way the world is, but that it is that is mystical."

The radio 3 presenter, Tom Service, writes in the *Guardian* that the last 'cataclysmically' slow movement of Mahler's Ninth Symphony "is one of the most famously death haunted places in orchestral music, a moment in which the music slowly, achingly, bridges the existential gap between sound and silence, presence and absence, life and death. The very last bar is even marked pianissimo, with a long pause—'ersterbend' (dying) as if its message wasn't already clear enough."

Leonard Bernstein, who felt this symphony keenly, believed that it captured personal death—of Mahler's daughter and his own mortality—and the mass deaths of world wars on the horizon. What follows is silence.

Particularly moving for me, bearing in mind the financial straits Kit was in at his end, was reading about Beethoven's circumstances as he flogged his unfinished *Missa Solemnis Mass* to multiple publishers as he battled ill health and debts. The composer's final words were "applaud friends, the comedy is ended."

Also, quoted as his publisher turned up with bottles of wine: "Pity, pity, too late."

What music, and the language of the Psalms can bring, is what Vaughan Williams described as "the glimpses of the heart of things which the composer has crystallised into earthly sound."

Rutter has said that he enters a spiritual state while he is composing and owes his musical style to his Christian heritage:

"In my memory, I have all those psalms and prayers and more than hundred hymns that can only be erased by death. Almost all the musicians I know are comfortable with the mysterious and the transcendental because music itself works in mysterious ways."

I partly understand what John Rutter means. I found poetic antithesis easier for a troubled heart than journalistic enquiry. Sorrow and darkness will finally be joined to light and joy, although the sorrow and darkness will always be there.

Haydn said the words 'let there be light' came straight from heaven. During a performance of his *Creation* in 1808, the audience applauded to the line:

'And God said Let there be light: And there was light.'

Haydn looked up and said: "Not from me, everything comes from up there."

The holy against the physical. I find the words 'everything comes from up there' comforting, running my hand over Kit's plain oak coffin, chosen by my sister, with the loose white and blue flowers, signifying the Cornish coast, which he loved.

The song my daughter-in-law thought right for Kit's funeral was:

O nata Lux by Tallis:

O light born of Light,
Jesus, redeemer of the world
With loving kindness deign to receive
Suppliant praise and prayer.
Thou who once deigned to
Be clothed in flesh
For the sake of the lost
Grant us to be members of thy blessed body.

Kit had already chosen the songs closest to him when he was interviewed by the Cam newspaper about being a choral scholar in 1975.

He picked first John Rutter's *Shepherd's Pipe Carol*

"He was barely older than us and was an enchantingly modest man. This piece of music was the start of the ascension of Clare's choir."

(Clare College was the first Cambridge College to admit girls, which boosted its academic success as well as its musical quality).

Stephen Sondheim's *Being Alive*

"This song will make you cry. It is about yearning for love and the nuisance of living with someone (Someone to hold you too close, someone to hurt you too deep) but how the alternative—being alone—is not being alive."

"The lyrics are flawless, it's accompanied by a gentle bossa nova and I learned something about the way words and music intersect. I was learning from being a chorister that I wouldn't be a singer, but I could re-write lyrics to make the choristers corpse. I could write libretti and maybe one day, I would write lyrics. I didn't know then that I would go on to study under Sondheim and would feel his loss deeply."

Thomas Tallis' *Spem in Alium*

"During my third year, the choir went on a spring tour that included Venice. We had fashion ideas by then—my friend and nemesis, Simon Butteriss, and I went around dressed as Tadzio in *Death and Venice*. We were guests of the British Council and the idea of the tour was to sing in the buildings the music had been written for. No one cared but we music nerds loved it."

"In the Basilica San Marco, we were in one of the domes singing Thomas Tallis's piece for forty voices and it was so beautiful, I needed to hear it, not to sign it, so I feigned a headache and sneaked downstairs where I bumped into the Pope. It was John Paul 1, I think. He was sitting in an apse. He saw me and winked and tapped his nose."

Gilbert and Sullivan's *When the Night Wind Howls*

"I had gone to the Minack Theatre in Cornwall with the Cambridge Gilbert and Sullivan Society. We were sleeping on the floor of a school and by the end of the trip, everyone had slept with everyone else and no one was speaking to anyone. It was wonderful."

It is a snapshot of Kit's musical world, from high church to vaudeville, and licentiousness. But he spoke little about spirituality until towards his end, during his collaboration with Roderick Williams and his musical bond with my daughter-in-law, Anna.

Did he know towards the end—as his daughter, Gus, thought he did—and what solace was it that his final work was religious, *The Vision of the Cross*?

It is Thomas Mann again: The grim physical reality of death, versus its metaphysical beauty.

For the great musicians, their sense of mortality became part of their music. Beethoven is said to have written without resting place notes in his final compositions. It was as if music floated into a place beyond the finish.

Francis Steele, the bass singer, particularly known for Bach said: "At the inconclusive conclusion of The Art of Fugue when the scratching of Bach's pen ceases and it falls from his fingers, when the triumphantly assembled lines evaporate into silence, there I approach closest to both mortality and the divine."

George Steiner, the Jewish intellectual who wrote that "much of my work has concerned itself, directly or indirectly, with trying to understand, to articulate, causal and teleological aspects of the Holocaust," saw the finality of death conveyed in Schubert's C Major quintet, the slow movement.

For me as for many others, Handel's *Messiah II* oratorio and particularly the text of *He Was Despised*, from Isaiah 53.3 is the best way to understand desolation as a human experience and answers the question of God's place in human suffering. Beauty and sadness. Silence between.

He was despised,
Despised and rejected
Rejected of men
A man of sorrows
A man of sorrows
And acquainted with grief.

I cannot find a greater piece of work about desolation. It shows the limits of scientific rationalism. Grief and mystery are part of the human experience and Handel, or Bach, can show what lies beyond the grave. Science and faith may indeed be part of the same rather than opposites.

Even the great Austrian logician, Kurt Godel, called his faith 'rationalistic, idealistic, optimistic and theological':

"I am convinced of this (the afterlife) independently of any theology. It is possible today to perceive by pure reasoning, that it is entirely consistent with known facts."

I dare not yet try this out on my friends at the Science Museum, where I am a trustee, but the mystery of death seems to me best expressed by faith and worst, reductively, by science. The shedding of cells is an explanation but not the poetry of the human condition. And there is something too brisk about the discussion of artificial intelligence when we have not yet worked out the nature of the human soul. As John Rutter says, are we asking the right questions?

The priest at Kit's funeral was also a friend of his, is chaplain at Hatfield House and has a home on the Norfolk coast.

After the funeral, I wrote to him to ask if I might come to see him because I was trying to understand Kit better. His death left me with a series of clues which included music, pilgrimages and nature. It sounded pretentious to say that left with the watery mass of Kit's brain, I was looking for the contours of his soul.

On a hot, tinder dry day, I drove into the estate parkland and found his home and bounding dogs, waist high to me. I had just seen some breaking news on my phone. The hiker who had found Julian on Mount Baldy gave details of his remains and the particulars of clothing found with him. Julian was identified by a driving licence in his pocket. The material and banal details of death. Henry believed that his father's soul remained on the mountain.

The priest and I sat looking at the formal gardens and feeding expensive soft cheese to the dogs. I talked to him about pilgrim routes, and cathedrals and Ely lake, a confident itinerary of legacy planning, undermined by my wobbling voice and spilling tears.

He listened, chose some anecdotes to illustrate Kit's sensitivity and liturgical knowledge, and offered to help me pull singing/pilgrimages/nature together. In other words, he was guiding me from sorrow to, sometime in the future, joy.

If this were the Canterbury pilgrimage, this would have been the priest's tale.

The experience of music and the church became closer the next day when I went to the 15th century Anglo Catholic St Mary's Church South Creake in north Norfolk, to watch the Ora Singers, directed by Suzi Digby.

The choir was viewed by the wooden carvings of angels looking down from the roofs and the bats flying out from the rafters during the monastic plainchant of Ave Verum Corpus, sung from the sides of the church. We need not labour the comparison between disembodied voices and heavenly hosts but it is a choreography I have noted since in Anna's Cambridge Voices choir performance at her local Bodney Church in Norfolk and the Christmas procession at Norwich Cathedral. You do not need to see to believe.

The service at South Creake was a celebration of William Byrd, for the singers claimed in the programme that we are in a new golden age of choral music 'matching that of the Renaissance'.

Byrd's most famous *Ave Verum Corpus* was sung off stage, the sopranos from Ora Singers gathered at the edges of the nave, their voices soaring to the angels on the roof.

Hail the true body, born of/from the Virgin Mary
You who truly suffered and were sacrificed on the
Cross for the sake of man.
From whose pierced flank flowed water and blood
Be a foretaste for us in the trial of death.
O sweet, O gentle,
O Jesu, son of Mary, have mercy on me

For those of faith, the answer to desolation, in shattering war or every day loss, is the cry of the crucifixion. "My God, My God, why hast thou forsaken me?"

I thought of Kit's lowest moments in his final months, when the odds were stacked up against him, loss of family life, home, future, his increasingly reckless disregard for his own health, and could see that these were also his moments of spiritual depth. There is no such thing as an ex-chorister.

One of his happiest messages in October 2022 was to his musical partner, James McConnel, who had composed the music to Kit's Cantata, in memory of Olaf Schmid, a George Cross recipient killed in Afghanistan in 2009.

Kit had found a moment of friendship with the bomb disposal sergeant whom he encountered surfing on a Cornish beach in 2008; he was intrigued to discover that Olaf Schmid was a former chorister at Truro Cathedral as well as a soldier.

It had taken James McConnel years before he was ready to put music to Kit's words because James's beautiful son, Freddy, had died tragically from drugs in 2011 and James could not face composing a Requiem.

But three months before Kit's death, James suddenly felt inspired and sent his work to Kit. Kit replied, copied to me, "Astonishing, James. It never ceases to amaze me how exponentially music enhances mere words."

On the cusp of suffering and death, the music rises. The Requiem from the Cantata was sung at Kit's funeral, the parts of Olaf Schmid's widow and son taken by my cousin, Naomi, and her daughter, Morwenna. This was a month after Kit's death.

And then just a week after his death, his anthem, *The Vision of the Cross*, with music by Roderick Williams, was performed at Magdalene Chapel for the processional Cross of the Cosmos.

I have found it hard since to separate the experience of sacred music from desolation and death. My God, My God, why hast thou forsaken me?

By coincidence, the music of Tallis and Byrd, the familiar English sacred music, dear to me through my daughter-in-law's choral singing with Cambridge Voices, was also composed during the Reformation, the schism with Rome a source of anguish for the Catholic believer William Byrd. Death and separation, the tearing apart of the woven tapestry of our worlds.

It was Bach who much later became known for counterpoint, dissonance, and beauty at the same time, but this tension is in our hearts and souls as part of our human experience.

Sacred music can acknowledge our deepest turmoil and somehow produce transcendent peacefulness.

And it is composers who seem to bridge the divide.

The composers who meant most to Kit, the chorister, were probably Charles Villiers Stanford, Hubert Parry, and Herbert Howells. I confess that I had not heard of any of them and their sensitivities to mortality were new to me.

The biographer of the 20th century British composer Herbert Howells, Paul Spicer, puts it like this: "Death is a transfiguration. In dying, composers, like writers and artists, leave a key to their souls, through which they live on, furthering the notion of immortality."

Music seems to be part of the river in The *Pilgrim's Progress*, words by John Bunyan, music by Vaughan Williams, flowing between life and death. Christian is overwhelmed by 'the sorrows of death' and does not think he will see land again. Hopeful replies:

"Be of good cheer, my brother, for I feel the bottom (of the river) and it is firm."

We sang *He would be Valiant Be*—Bunyan's words—at Kit's cremation and it was sung again at Julian's school memorial.

The hymn has power because of its stoicism in the face of the sorrow of death, not despite it.

Howells' life seemed to me a river of sorrow:

His contemporaries fought and some were killed in the Great War including Francis Purcell Warren 'Bunny', a viola player for whom Howells wrote the Elegy for viola sola, string quartet. He wept in front of a photograph of Bunny on his mantelpiece.

Then, there was the death of his son, Michael, described in a staccato diary entry which conveys the sheer terror of losing him during three days of a summer holiday in Gloucestershire in 1935.

Wednesday 4: Mick's coming to our room in early morning. Temperature. Bad back. Dr Nanda sent for.

Thursday 5: Mick worse. Dr N at 11.15. Orders for London. Ambulance and Cheltenham Flier—London—Dr Dowling. Nursing Home. Dr Hunt. Fearful anxiety.

Friday 6: Nursing home at 8.45—Dr H at 9 am. With M most of the morning—lunch with Scotts. M again at 2.30. Grave change. Mrs Fisher came—Mick worse, always. Dr H 7 pm.

Hope, then despair. Dr Brunton. Dr Fisher. Mick died at 10.10 pm.

Herbert Howells' daughter, Ursula, remembered Michael turning 'bluey black' as his lungs ceased to function. He had a virulent form of polio.

The desolate sadness of the burial is also addressed in timetable form:

"They came for Mick at 8.30 am and we watched him set out for Gloucestershire and Peace. Agony by road through Oxfordshire and over the Cotswolds."

"We followed by 10.45 train from Paddington and went straight to Twigworth and took gentle leave of him."

Howells' famous requiem work, *Hymnus Paradisi*, ends in eternal light.

"Holy is the true light and passing wonderful, lending radiance to them that endure in the heat of the conflict."

He confronted death in its most terrible forms—war and the death of a child—yet it was not the end.

Grief becomes mournful beauty although never resolved. At the end of his life, he said: "I don't believe there is anything," and yet cathedral music was a religious endeavour.

And he did not turn his back on an afterlife.

His diary entry for October 1936 is quoted in Paul Spicer's book:

"During the night of Monday and Tues., I dreamed of Mick. He sat on my knee looking well and happy and was quietly affectionate. He said: 'I am not really gone from you. I am with you always.'"

The spiritual influence of cathedrals is something I am keeping an eye on. The former Labour Chancellor, Ed Balls, showed a dedication to Herbert Howells which was clearly baffling to his podcast partner and former Conservative Chancellor, George Osborne.

Balls broke off from discussion of high political drama in order to tell Osborne that he was more interested in his radio 3 assignment to conduct a work by Herbert Howells.

Of course! Ed Balls's father lives in Norwich Cathedral close. Evensong is part of Balls's spiritual life.

There is something about the mournful beauty of cathedrals and Evensong, the river of sorrow and firm ground beneath that captures the atmosphere of bereavement.

A shocking death can feel like a private war, mind and emotions torn to pieces. It perhaps made me more sensitive to the real flesh and blood horror of the Ukraine war, the many thousands of amputees, the numbing of sensibilities, the never ending grief of mothers.

Kit's childhood was spent singing at funerals, at Canterbury Cathedral and he was drawn back to the theme. His idea of a Cantata for Olaf Schmid, soldier and chorister, drew together the most piquant themes of war, lost youth, purity of voice.

Kit's musical partner, James McConnel, responsible for the music, used a cello as the voice of Olaf Schmid, and a treble to represent the pure voice of his young step son. The treble voice, the innocent child, war, death. Then, the very last thing Kit wrote before he died, his anthem for *Vision of the Cross*, spoke of 'dust reordered, dust we may restore'. It is a variation on Requiem Aeternum.

I searched for a reading at Kit's funeral and I know now why my friend, the theatre director Sir Nicholas Hytner, suggested to me the poem by Elizabeth Bishop, *I am in Need of Music:* It answers the jaggedness of fretfulness with a yearning for melody 'deep, clear and liquid slow'.

It presents music as healing waters. The verse which washed over me speaks of "a spell of rest, and quite breath and cool heart that sinks through fading colours deep/To the subaqueous stillness of the sea, and floats forever in a moon green pool/held in the arms of rhythm and of sleep."

Reading this felt to me like a more lyrical version of plain chant, pure and still. It is Bunyon's river of sorrow, while feeling the firm ground beneath.

One modern healer is a curly headed, lean, youthful figure a couple of years older than my brother, Kit. I make the comparison because he was a Canterbury Cathedral chorister at the same time. His name is Harry Christophers and he is the founder and conductor of the sacred music singers, The Sixteen.

He met me at the train station near his home in Otford Kent. I think of him conducting in formal black but he is actually wearing shirt and shorts. We ate a salad lunch with his intellectually sharp wife, looking out over his garden and then the expanse of South Down.

We grimaced about the conditions of gardening in chalk soil and marvelled over the bird identifying app Merlin. It felt all rolling hills and no abyss here, but Harry had a kind of emotional short hand.

When I mentioned that I was starting a conservation project at a lake in sight of Ely Cathedral, he gave me a sideways look of gentlest sympathy and gasped: "A view of Ely! How wonderful."

He understood how very sad I was and stirred me towards the heavenly shape of a cathedral. He also told me that choirs tended to avoid Ely because it was so cold. I decided not to tell Anna, because I wanted to bring her choir Cambridge Voices to sing a concert in memory of Kit.

Harry Christophers pondered the closeness of music and faith. He said that audiences who have listened, especially to Bach, will say:

"I don't believe in God, I don't believe there's a heaven, but if I did, I have been there."

"I find that absolutely staggering. And that just shows I think that everybody has a spiritual side and the music that we perform brings that out in them."

"And we have seen more people turning to this music to get some sort of relief, or fulfilment, to take away the trials of a difficult day, or because they have bereavements or troubles in their lives."

He glanced at me tactfully.

Comfort to troubled hearts.

Even the atheist Nietzsche recognised the power of music to transcend. He wrote: "Without music, life would be a mistake. The German imagines God as a songster."

Music as an expression of heaven has some ancient pedigree. It is the sublime order of justice and peace.

For Dante, the medieval Italian poet and philosopher, the sixth sphere of heaven was the home of history's just rulers, now transformed into singing stars.

Music was the means to apprehend God. It is an expression of awe.

Sacred music came from the monasteries as a form of prayer and then as it became more layered and complex moved to the cathedrals and the universities.

My preferred Sunday worship is Evensong at one of the Cambridge colleges, open to the public and purer than a Sunday service.

Harry Christophers reminded me that while this tradition of music was originally written as an accompaniment to liturgy, it has taken a different turn.

It was for the glory of God. Now it is performed in concert halls. If it is separated from liturgy, then what makes it still sacred?

I ventured the John Rutter view that it is the mystery that is sacred.

Harry Christophers said: "Yes, even without believing in God, it would get me there. It is unlike just other lovely music. I think a lot about the language."

"A lot of the pieces are in Latin. Nobody speaks Latin today but somehow the beauty of the vowels, just the beauty of the language is affecting."

"There is a danger when the Anglican church says everything needs to be in English—a return now to real music, with substance."

It is this belief which lies behind the choral pilgrimage, set up by Harry Christophers in 2000. They can attract a thousand people to York Minister. Yet there is one spot for Sunday classical music on BBC 4. Come on!

One of the wicked mistakes of Covid was the silencing of choral singing. Imagine, the country needing spirituality more than ever and the doors of churches close.

In an answer to this yearning, Harry Christophers filmed a choral odyssey, set in big houses or chapels with singers socially distanced and a presenter, Simon Russell Beale, in conversation from yards away. Human distance in order to achieve choral unison. Hatfield House featured prominently, the former palace of the Bishop of Ely. It is now the home of the Cecil family, who are patrons of sacred music and of The Sixteen in particular.

The first programme was about William Byrd, serene compositions born out of anguish of forbidden faith. Harry Christophers also recorded a radio 3 programme on Byrd and Faith, in which his composition *Civitas Sancti Tui* is discussed.

It is a piece about desolation and loss, Jerusalem deserted, Sion deserted. The music is homophonic, still and dark and deep.

By coincidence, I had wandered into St Etheldreda Church, Ely Place in Holborn a few weeks before seeing Harry Christophers. I did not know then of its relationship to Hatfield House and to Ely Cathedral. St Etheldreda Church is linked to the St Etheldreda's Anglican parish church in Hatfield, where Kit's friend the priest preached. For she is a patron saint of the Bishops of Ely who once occupied Hatfield House before Henry V111 seized it.

I had time to kill before a business meeting, and it was on my mind that it was the day of Julian's small funeral in LA and I was very much hoping that Henry and his step-mother and sisters would find some peace of mind.

I sent Henry an iPhone picture of the serene stone and wood chapel with its astonishingly bright stained glass window behind the altar.

I had not realised until Harry told me, that this was the Catholic sanctuary for William Byrd. *Civitus Sancti Tui* seems to be a perfect expression of human desolation over loss. Jerusalem deserted. That music, those words in this place.

In Harry's choral odyssey, he paired Byrd with a composer four hundred years later, the Estonian Arvo Part who stood up for his faith against Soviet tyranny.

Part defied inhuman brutality with the compositional purity of bells. It is called Tintinnabuli and is based on plain chant. It is described as holy minimalism and is extraordinarily profound. It is the sound of peace, the sound we all hope will come once the hateful Russian aggression in Ukraine ends. I have since listened more to Avo Part and his profoundly beautiful and sorrowful music. Spiegel im Spiegel is one of the better known pieces in which Part describes the piano as the guardian angel to the song of the cello. It sounds to me like a musical pilgrimage.

Sorrow and joy, whether Bach, Beethoven or Benjamin Britten expresses both the inevitability of death and the musical transcendence. There is indeed a music just for this, which is the Requiem.

After Kit died, his musical partner, James McConnel, persevered to stage the Cantata and Requiem that he and Kit had written.

It seemed fateful that it was not performed during Kit's lifetime because it had taken on an even deeper meaning, a combination of sorrows flowing into a piece of music about war itself, the worst kind of collective death.

I shall write of Kit's Requiem in a later chapter, and of the masters of the form. For me, this has been a journey of understanding, of Kit, and of sorrow and joy, a journey without endings, until one equal end. Life is more mysterious than we acknowledge.

I am not a musician and can only listen. But as Rowan Williams said:

"To listen seriously to music and to perform it are among our most potent ways of learning what it is to live with and before God."

This is what Augustine felt present in the Psalms. "It unseals deep places, emotions otherwise buried."

It is in those deep places that we can find the heart of things.

Chapter 2
Cathedrals and Choristers

Kit as a senior chorister at Canterbury Cathedral.

Sir Tim Rice words to an extra verse of *God Rest You Merry Gentlemen*, December 2023.

God Rest Kit Hesketh-Harvey
Your passing caused dismay
The saints and sinners choristers
Are all in disarray
However will we ever cope without
Your shining wit today
Your tidings of comfort and joy
Comfort and joy
How we miss you and your comfort and joy.

My posthumous trail of Kit is a tale of cathedrals. Kit was a chorister at Canterbury and came to love Ely and Norwich Cathedrals as I learned to. When the police gave me the key to the vestry in Stoke Ferry, church Norfolk, which had become Kit's home, I found an inhabited room with a terrible absence; his packed small suitcase for a film festival he never got to, neat belongings, and in the church itself, an easel with some amateur water colourings on the floor, gathering dust and trampled underfoot.

One was of the lake at Ely, with the unmistakeable silhouette of the cathedral at the far end. It was the view which I had described to Kit's fellow chorister, Harry Christophers, and which had made him gasp in recognition. Ely Cathedral is described as the 'ship of the fens' but to Kit, it would have been a mother ship.

He was brought up with the ghosts of history, a thousand years of song, sliding between the temporal and the spiritual. His daughter, Gus, said of Kit in her funeral eulogy that he taught her to step between worlds. She was talking about the magic of theatre but it had an ethereal resonance too. The light and shadows and language of the cathedrals were part of him. As John Rutter said, there is no such thing as an ex-chorister.

After Kit's funeral, his fellow choristers held their own reunion, because what would non-choristers know of their shared existence?

As for the architectural merit of the cathedrals, I defer to Simon Jenkins's book on cathedrals which rates Ely and Canterbury highly. I am competitive and, in my past journalistic career, have felt exultant if I have beaten another newspaper with a scoop. This is nothing next to my pride on seeing Ely about YORK in Simon's ratings.

As for Canterbury, Simon Jenkins writes:

"I came to regard Canterbury, in almost every respect, as the noblest church in England. It has a depth, a variety of appeal that can absorb the visitor for a day and some visitors for a life. I remain in awe of its status as a history book in stone."

He also writes:

"I once sat in Yevele's Perpendicular Nave on a spring afternoon and watched the sun's rays wander back and forth through the arcades as a choir rehearsed Mozart's C-minor mass. It was an unforgettable marriage of sight and sound."

I had also sat in the nave in childhood on visits to hear Kit sing. And then, when Kit died, I found some sheets of lined A4 paper, mixed with childhood letters to him from me and my sister, Jojo, with his description of life at the cathedral.

I cannot tell exactly what age he wrote it but I reckon it was early teenage so retrospective but close enough to feel authentic. There is a homoerotic yearning which remained with Kit through his life but hidden from public because of the reticence of the social stigma of his times somehow combined with a high church respect for the sanctity of the institution of marriage.

This is what he wrote:

"Dawn came up over the cathedral. Grey. The dawn amongst the stones was always grey, brooding, almost unnoticeable. What had earlier seemed a massive, motherly, parapeted blackness was now slowly, so slowly, diffused with an imperceptible paleness."

"Nothing stirred, or awoke, but the towers and transepts and buttresses and precincts evolved into relief and shadow, form and void, arch, column, sheer wall. Like a monstrous flower unfolding, but gentle."

"The presence of the cathedral was the central feature of the lives of all those within its shadow. Consciously, or subconsciously, it formed the pivot point of their environment, their existence. Too cold and colossal to be a person, it was nevertheless too dominant to be considered a mere building."

"It lived and breathed in the people around it. It was their mother, womb, and their mother breast. And when they slept, it slept. Only now, the larger context of the universe, of day and night, became dominant once more."

"The precinct dwellers slept, oblivious of dawn and dusk. Their existence dwindled to insignificance. For an hour or so, the cathedral lived a detached existence a life—if this slow dawn could be called life—of its own. The people who lived around it, carried out their duties within it, worshipped in it and fed off it safe in its security, its omnipotent shadow, these slept while the dawn seeped in."

"And now dawn came up over the cathedral. Even the city was silent and unseen. The dark, medieval streets, dusty and narrow, lay wrapped in the closeting silence. The old alms-houses and shops, the half-timbered gables, the shuttered porches and the single burning lights, noiseless, suspended, very still."

"At a precinct window, a boy brooded as the dawn camp up. He was shivering slightly in the morning coolness and moved closely around him the functional striped flannel pyjama jacket. He was not watching the dawn, not even when the grey was suffused with the palest hint of gold and crimson. His strange, heavy lidded, sea-green eyes were glazed, abstracted, strangely bright for the morning."

"Beautiful eyes, strikingly serene and veiled. Sea-green. His chin rested thoughtfully on his hand, leaning out from the window ledge, his mouth pouting slightly into the silence and the dew and the still grey stone. For a moment, he closed the wild green eyes shuddered silently drunk the cold dawn air. Then without moving, he opened his eyes again and resumed the abstracted stare."

"The light was not yet vivid enough to catch the glossy auburn in his thick chestnut hair or the strange darkness of his skin. For the while, both were suffused in the deadening, uniform grey, which dulled the colouring into silence and he watched, heavy lidded, dark lashed brooding."

"There was a strange defiance in his face, a smouldering, insolent pride which showed in the intense eyes, the sulky mouth, the resolute boy's chin. He could not be aged more than thirteen or fourteen but smacked of southern princelings, of fiery natures and untameable arrogance. The light could not hide even that."

"Behind him, a darkened room, heavy and warm, and close with sleeping boys. Now and then a rustling of hot sheets, a creaking spring, an unconscious sigh. The strange noises of night, darkness even at dawn. The boy was unaware of all these, of darkness and well as dawn. His bed was beside him, the bedclothes crumpled and tousled, the sheets a ghostly pale grey that leapt through the darkness. Most of the several boys in the dormitory slept with the blankets off, shrouded in a similar whiteness, which became progressively duskier as the room receded. They were all asleep."

"Still, the boy watched. There was still silence. Not even the birds in the great precinct elms had begun to sing. The dawn continued, five minutes, ten, twenty. The city began to breathe, and then to hum. The boy hadn't moved. The shadows of the cathedral were obvious, now suddenly. He could see everything—the brick work, the tracery, the most intricate masonry. The golden pinnacles on the central tower had begun to shine weakly."

"The bell struck. Six o'clock. The reverberations crashed through the silence, booming, resonating, slowly, inevitably. The boy blinked at the tower, and counted the strokes. No one else moved, or stirred even but the boy came alive. He stared at the colossal, weighty tower, rearing up into the grey dawn sky. He let his arm drop. Somehow, the starlings had begun to sing shrilly."

"The last stroke throbbed away, taking minutes—or was it only seconds? To die into silence. The boy stood up, stretched, looked back over his shoulder into the room. They were still sleeping."

"Then, he padded softly over to the penultimate bed. The floorboards, old and oaken, were tacky beneath his feet. Someone stretched and turned over his sleep. The boy froze, counted to sixty. Then to seventy-five. Then, the dawn shining onto his green and white pyjamas he glided swiftly, softly to within an inch of his roommate's pillow."

"What it was that was so magical about Matthew Davenport none of us at the cathedral school could define; but it was a magic of which were all very much aware. Our knowledge of his background was limited. He had joined us half-way from another school which had closed down for reasons which we never did manage to establish."

"We were precocious and self-assertive twelve year olds were at first wary, and then curious about this handsome green-eyed newcomer with the singing voice that made fountains weep, and the aloof detachment of a foreign princeling."

"We were all told of his imminent arrival, that he would be singing the Laudate Dominium solo that evening in the cathedral. Those who had wanted to sing that particular solo themselves were resentful, the remainder curious and amazed that the choirmaster should allocate this coveted and demanding solo to a complete stranger."

"We glimpsed him after choir practice that evening, robing along in the choir vestry before Evensong. Subconsciously, if not consciously sensitive to his good looks, we were all somewhat taken aback by his appearance, brief through an encounter with him was. The dark skin, dark auburn curls, the lazy green eyes contrasted strikingly with the intense whiteness of his surplice."

"Most of us felt undefined empathy with him, a spiritual reaching out towards him, frail, tender through this human response was it sowed the seeds of later passion."

"He turned to look at us as we processed past him in silence. His pride and command had given way, momentarily, to a frightened half smile of nervous acknowledgement. His lips were finely drawn but the smile did not suit him. I smiled back and instantly his face resumed its sulking defiance."

"The choirmaster took him away to the High Altar before any of us could speak to him. He knew nothing about him, forgot about him, even. We robed in the normal way. The leaders among us grouped in a close, jealous huddle and talked. Others combed their hair in silence, minds away from the waiting cathedral, or the gentle organ music that filtered through. It was a Friday evening; there would be a large congregation."

"Processing in, down the north aisle, watched by the memorial stone saints on either side, in a careful double column every boy's thought wandered. Waiting behind the High Altar, I remember thinking that completely along in the cavernous east end of the cathedral is the new boy."

"He was waiting probably hideously nervous. The autumn light was washing the nave with evening. The stone glows softly in a colossal series of massive columns all the way down to the great West Door. The stained glass gave an atmosphere of unreality to the light in that nave, to the little side chapels in particular."

"It danced on the tracery. The silent presence of the cathedral awaited us."

"As we entered in a blinding burst of white surplices and glittering silver and pall, the organ swelled: we fell to our appointed places, an unconscious solemnity on every face, a small thrill of pride and pleasure in every heart. The service began, as it had begun every night like this for centuries. We were hardly aware of its progress but sang as we had been trained to do, sometimes grinning at each other, something exchanging the half smiling glances of those who shared each other's beds."

"We were all looking forward to Laudate Dominum for boys' voices only and ineffably tender and sweet as Mozart's perfection alone could express. The phrases, like delicately wrought, but strongly based arches, suited the Gothic sweeps and curves of the cathedral, blended somewhere into it. And at the raised end of the cathedral, silent and at a vast distance from where we were, a boy was waiting."

"That first long phrase of his, unfolding like a clean silver flower, poised, pure, yet with a strength behind it that sent it leaping down the length of the cathedral brought us up like a draught of icy water. The candles burned silently, distantly, mistily as ever on the cream and gold altar cloth; the candlelight in the darkened sanctuary made the whole area of the building seem detached."

"We'd noticed the effect a thousand times and had all been spiritually moved by it, but now, from that holy of holies a handsome boy was singing the Laudate more clearly, more effortlessly, more·beautifully than ever before. None of us could see him, we could only this hear transcendent voice bounding off the vaults and arches a hundred yards away from singing to perfection to us. Some of us frowned in surprise and concentration. Some of us gasped, transfixed, smiling in wonder."

"The heads of the choir and the congregation all turned in that one direction, attentive to that one mellifluous voice, that solitary, unknown boy."

"And when the rest of the voices came in, echoing in unison that same opening phrase, only gold not silver, the choirmaster wept with joy at our simple enunciation and the music's magical beauty."

There you have it, a closed world, homoerotic boyish ardour, the cathedral mother, and an understanding of the musically sublime.

Harry Christophers was a day boy so removed from the puberty sexual awakening of the dormitory but the experience of cathedral singing remained with him. He said:

"I remember when I was first a chorister at Canterbury Cathedral and just how special that was. I remember the anthem *O Nata Lux* by Thomas Tallis."

"To sing that in Canterbury Cathedral as a ten or eleven year old, not realising that we had all this pressure on us really, but to be in the cassock and surplice, singing glorious music in the fantastic acoustic was wonderful. That's remained with me forever. It was where we worked and played, our prints were there. We would cycle round ancient oaks."

He went on: "When we're performing in beautiful cathedrals and abbeys, through listening to the music, people really begin to realise that these buildings were built with this music in mind and the composers wrote with the building in mind and that simple hand in glove idea is significant. So we know what the sounds are like, we know the architecture, the phrases the way it just feels reacting to the stone work or the stained glass window. That is an incredible realisation."

And perhaps history and religion are part of the same. The Conservative philosopher Roger Scruton wrote that living in the present is an irreligious concept.

He wrote that the postmodern world has "become deaf to the voice of absent generations and lives in the thin time slice of the now…In such a condition it is inevitable that people should lose all sense of a sacral community so as to become locked in the isolation of their own desires."

Within a cathedral, the past is always present; Kit used to play hop scotch on the flag stones of the cloisters, which were also grave stones. It was not just the liturgy but the sacred architecture which he carried with him, into a career of bohemian cabaret. He satirised almost everything, but so far as religion was concerned, he only trained his sights on Leviticus.

His exuberant wit always stopped short of the nave.

John Rutter gave the esoteric example of Kit's sensitivity to the sacred, that Kit alone in an audience of experts, had been able to distinguish a piece of music written in the style of Charles Villiers Stanford, but actually by Rutter. This is not the kind of achievement that would light up the internet but it showed a seriousness which he tried hard to hide until his end.

He had a respect for musical traditions. Choral singing came out of the monasteries.

As composer Howard Goodall writes in his The Story *of Music*, what started as the monophonic sound of monastic plainchant changed when boys were added to the choir.

"The musical effect of adding the boys is that there are now two parallel lines of music, not just one, since the boys' voices are higher than those of the men. The higher version the boys sing is made up of identical notes to the men's but at a higher register; so there is a fixed, natural distance between the two identical lines of music. This fixed distance between a note and its higher self is something that occurs in nature…" This developed over centuries into harmonies. The Greek term for many voices, polyphonic.

Goodall credits one of the first named composers to take advantage of musical notation and to introduce lyricism in plainchant.

"A spectacularly clever and imaginative German woman, Hildegard of Bingen, who was born in 1098. She was also a scientist, nun, poet visionary and diplomat…Hildegard's imaginative, lyrical and reflective music represents a fulcrum between two eras. It still essentially sounds like a colourful variant of plainchant, but she embellished the outline of the tune with touches of her own."

Church music, particularly in France, became lovelier and more intricate at the same time that the Black Death swept through Europe.

Howard Goodall writes: "Alongside death and despair, this was also the period of astounding Gothic architecture, with the most extraordinary cathedrals, abbeys and churches being built all over Europe. To sing a note in one of these cavernous spaces is to hear its sound echo and reverberate, returning to its source, modified by the building itself."

Choral singing, particularly Evensong, is why the great cathedrals and abbeys draw in congregations. The call of the past is compelling. For those who have been brought up in the tradition, the stone moulds itself round them.

I found a social media entry by Edmund de Waal, remember, a son of a former dean of Canterbury, for Evensong at Ely in September 2023.

"Evensong yesterday in the Lady Chapel at Ely Cathedral—one of the most extraordinary medieval spaces in England, floating rhythms of stone and air, each sculpture of a saint broken in the Reformation."

"The official first day of autumn—deep shadows in the cathedral and the chapel full of shifting light."

"Evensong has been sung here in one form or another for a thousand years—last night sung beautifully by a choir from all over the world."

I savour this description, because I have managed to book the Lady Chapel at Ely for a post Easter 2024 concert by Anna's choir Cambridge Voices. The title is Byrd and Bird—spirituality and nature. Kit's priest will give an introduction. He says the prevailing impression of the Lady Chapel is the astonishing light.

It cannot but define you to be a child brought up in a cathedral. I have a rough idea now of the choristers in public life and I identify them when opportunities arise. The shadow foreign secretary, David Lammy, is speaking at science and politics summit which I co-run in Braemar in Scotland. I walk him down the street from the hotel to the village hall venue, where he is preparing to talk on the geopolitical landscape.

But what about the cathedral landscape?

I ask him, entirely out of the blue, if he thinks much about his time as a chorister at Peterborough Cathedral.

He answers delightedly and without surprise, that of course he does, and he urges me to seek out his old choir master. His final words before going on stage are:

"And will you be writing about cathedral organs?"

Similarly, the Channel 4 former news anchor, Jon Snow, softens when I interrupt our media discussion for his podcast to ask him about his time as a chorister. His father was a bishop and his mother a pianist who studied at the Royal College of Music. Jon is known for a distinguished award winning journalistic career reporting from trouble spots, and also perhaps for shouting 'fuck the Tories' at Glastonbury. But his training as a chorister at Winchester Cathedral is less known.

Our conversation about the merits of Herbert Howells, Henry Purcell, and William Byrd becomes so animated and lengthy that the producer starts signalling to us in alarm to return to earthly concerns of media impartiality. But Jon's eyes are shining. What is there to say about Ofcom when the music floods back from the choir stalls?

"I think it's the essence of expression. And I think as a child, you learn about cadence, emphasis, crescendo. These are things which kind of inform your life from then on and you know very well when you have over crescendoed and perhaps when you have under diminuendoed."

"For those five or six years, you are drenched in someone else's view of what you should be doing, in terms of articulation. You learn so much about your relationship with the building, with the acoustics. The other thing is that I was very thick. And I was no good at sport. But I could sing."

"Oh! I loved the architecture of it. And it was rather sweet because although I wasn't close to my father, my parents took a camper van nearby so that they could see me sing. I was so embarrassed."

And it gave me a link which went beyond the building, through my whole life. It was a lovely, lovely start.

Three o'clock in the afternoon and on a Sunday.

I ask him if he considers himself religious.

"I go to church. But I wouldn't call myself religious. I would say I like being part of a community. I like to be there in a body of humanity."

The cathedrals were first imagined as a bridge between heaven and earth: Heaven on Earth is the title Emma J Wells chose for her book about cathedrals. It was the original purpose of Abbot Suger the 11th century abbot who supervised the rebuilding of St Denis Cathedral, outside Paris, in the Gothic style, on which all the cathedrals that I love best are based. They were churches of enormous light through stone and rose windows.

The ambition of stone masons was vaulting, to go as high as the architecture would allow. The Gothic style of the Middle Ages, starting in the 11th century, was the expression of this ambition. It set in stone the vision of hereafter and over the centuries, the treble voices of choristers seemed to be singing to God himself.

Dr Emma Wells writes: "These great, multi-faceted buildings were attempts to make the spiritual concrete while also representing symbolic voyages between this world and the next. …In particular, the Gothic style of cathedral was intended to be the physical exemplar of the Celestial City, the Heavenly Jerusalem, following the Apocalypse, as described in the Book of Revelation."

She illustrates the claim by quoting first William Wordsworth's *Inside of King's College Chapel:*

Of nicely calculated less or more;
So deemed the man who fashioned for the sense
These lofty pillars, spread that branching roof
Self-poised, and scooped into ten thousand cells,
Where light and shade repose, where music dwells
Lingering, and wandering on as loth to die;
Like thoughts whose very sweetness yieldeth proof
That they were born for immortality

Followed by Revelation 21:1–4

…high Heaven rejects the lore
And I saw a new heaven and a new earth;
For the first heaven and the first earth were passed
Away;
And there was no more sea.
And I saw John from the holy city, the new Jerusalem,
Coming down from God out of heaven, prepared
As a bride adored for her husband…

And God shall wipe away all tears from their eyes.

Neither shall there be any more pain; for the former things are passed away.

As I followed the path Kit, intended or unintended, laid for me along the pilgrim and trade route from Norfolk to Germany to the Baltic Coast, I found monumentally high cathedrals even in modest market towns. The merchants who made fortunes believed that the glory should rest with God and took out an insurance policy on their souls.

After my father died, in 2022, a year before Kit, which was a great blessing, I went through his books in neat piles by his tweed reading arm chair in his sitting room. On top of the pile was one called *I Saw Eternity The Other Night*: Timothy Day on King's College Cambridge and an English singing style.

This seemed quite a claim, but it was a quote from the 17th century metaphysical poet, Henry Vaughan:

I saw Eternity the other night,
Like a great ring of pure and endless light,
All calm, as it was bright;
And round beneath it, Time in hours, days, years,
Driv'n by the spheres
Like a vast shadow mov'd; in which the world
And all her train were hurl'd...

It takes a lecturer on English cathedrals to reference eternity with such ease.

The book charts the life of the King's College Choir, which became synonymous with Christmas and a particular English tradition described by a critic in Gramophone magazine in 1934 as:

"The exquisite quality of its boys voices. In no other country have they the same ethereal purity and pathos."

John Ruskin, the 19th century philosopher and art critic, too, argued it was the combination of architecture and treble voices which made cathedral singing in a world of its own.

"The setting mattered. As Charles Wesley the (18th century) master of hymns, said: No coat of varnish can do for a picture what the exquisitely reverberating qualities of a cathedral can do for music."

The golden age for the high Anglican Church, which is where Kit felt most comfortable and which stirs me, was during the 19th century in what was called the Oxford Movement. Timothy Day writes of the "revival of ceremonial outward forms of medieval church. There was renewed interest in old music, in plainsong, and ancient polyphone, in carols, in liturgies and medieval liturgical practices."

A fellow of Magdalen College Oxford wrote a manual in 1848 called *The Devout Chorister* (I wish I had been able to pass on this publication to Kit and almost renamed this book).

"The vocation of a chorister, although of course inferior to that of a priest in ministerial power, is yet higher than that of a priest, so far as the odour of sanctity peculiar to childhood imparts a glory to the office which appertains to none other."

The sublimity is necessarily fleeting, which makes it all the more moving. The voices of the choristers break. I have a recording of Kit singing the part of the page in *Good King Wenceslas*, aged nine.

A choir master from St Paul's is quoted by Tim Day as saying that the boy's voices were at their best aged ten, after a year or more of training. They would never be as pure again. When girls joined choirs, they lacked this trauma of loss.

Timothy Day's book charts the anguished debate over the qualities of boys' and girls' voices but Kit had no doubts on this. At Clare College Cambridge, he was a member of the first mixed college choir, under John Rutter. It led both to competitive success and greater all round happiness.

Of course, choristers may have the voices of angels but they also had the habits of boys and some choir masters were more patient than others.

Day quotes the records of Arthur Henry Mann at Norwich 1864: "The daily regime at Norwich when he was a chorister is said to have followed this plan: 8.30 until 9.45 scales and exercises; 10 am to 11 am Matins; 11–12.30 school work; 2 pm to 3.45 rehearsal; 4 pm to 5 pm Evensong; 5 pm to 7 pm school work."

Different choir masters had different techniques for getting the best out of the boys.

There was a choir master at Norwich called Zechariah Buck who was determined that a boy should sing the word 'darkness' with genuine feeling:

"Thou has laid me in the lowest pit: in a place of darkness and the deep."

His method was to lock boys up in cupboards.

"Now," he shouted, "do you know what darkness is?"

"No, Sir," the little boy shouted back. "There's a great crack in the door and I can see quite well."

Sacred music and liturgy express death as peace. As Cardinal Newman pronounced it, "until the shadows lengthen and the evening comes and the busy world is hushed and the fever of life is over."

Turbulence against rest, fever versus stillness and most of all war ending in peace.

I had not realised how the Great War and our traditional Christmas service of Nine Lessons and Carols were entwined. It was created from the despair of what to offer those who had fought through blackness.

Eric Milner-White was an army chaplain on the Western Front and mentioned in Despatches, before becoming Dean of Chapel at King's College Cambridge. There, he introduced the service of Nine Lessons and Carols, broadcast by the BBC since 1928 and said to have originated at Truro Cathedral. The service associated with innocence and joy was created as an antidote to the horror of war.

The choir master and conductor most cited by Kit and Harry Christophers, and every other contemporary chorister is Sir David Willcocks, who directed the Choir of King's College Cambridge from 1957 to 1974, and who died in 2015.

He was director of music for the wedding of Prince Charles and Diana Spencer so also understood the occasion of music. We are all aware, consciously or not, of his presence every Christmas, because of his descant arrangements for *Once in Royal David's City*, and *O come, all ye faithful*, among others.

David Willcocks had also been awarded the Military Cross for bravery 1944 Normandy.

Furthermore, he played the organ at the funeral of his younger son, James. I reel at the thought of his discipline in grief.

John Rutter wrote of Willcocks: "David loved life, probably because he had witnessed so much tragic loss of it in the war, also, perhaps, from the loss of his son, James, at the age of thirty-three from cancer."

Listening to his descants at the Christmas Procession at Norwich Cathedral, in the year that Kit died, I am attuned to the obvious realisation that Christmas is sorrow as well as joy. We know how it ends. One of the carols sung by the Norwich Cathedral choir, music by Peter Warlock and words by Bruce Blunt, puts the two events sequentially in two verses:

Bethlehem Down is full of the starlight,
Winds for the spices, and stars for the gold,
Mary for sleep and for lullaby music,
Songs of a shepherd by Bethlehem fold.
When he is King they will clothe him in grave sheets,
Myrrh for embalming and wood for a crown,
He that lies now in the white arms of Mary,
Sleeping to lightly on Bethlehem Down…

The solemnity of the candle light reflected on stone, the procession of choristers, from the Eastern Chapel to the nave, one tiny, with spectacles covering most of his face, the flinging open of the West Door into the darkness and swirling mist of Norwich cloisters; it is overwhelmingly profound.

The appeal of architecture, aspiring to heaven and voices that seem to come from the ether is not hard to understand. It is why Ed Balls, David Lammy, Jon Snow and Harry Christophers, and generations of choristers experience choral singing in cathedrals so deeply.

Timothy Day quotes the Chapter at St Paul's who explained that silent cathedrals were "at best awesome monuments: fill them with music and you have one of the most potent keys of man's devising for unlocking his earthbound spirit."

Chapter 3
The Hanseatic Connection

Norfolk, where I live, has a network of waterways up to Cambridgeshire, which were once lively trading routes. In the other direction, Lincolnshire, which voted heavily for Brexit, was in the 14th century a cosmopolitan county, bustling with merchants from Norway, northern Germany, Holland, and Flanders, a place where corn, ale, lead, wool and cloth were shipped abroad and furs, hawks, iron, brass, millstones, marble, timber, wine, dye, spices, and fish were traded back across Hanseatic routes through Germany up to the Baltic states.

This was the age of the British wool trade: According to Hanseatic author, Paul Richards, an estimated nine million sheep were shorn in the 13th century to fill wool sacks.

Eight centuries later, we still talk of it in Norfolk. The consortium owners of a race horse in our village call themselves the Hanseatic League. We are more at home in the cold featureless North Sea than the warm waters of the Mediterranean. We like cod but know that mackerel and herring are more sustainable. We have left the German centric EU only to find an older alliance with the Hanseatic League, which is basically German.

The Lutheran Reformation had its effect on this part of Britain where ruined Catholic monasteries are challenged by Protestant zeal. In 1607, during the reign of King James I, the Separatists, a group of Puritans with Lincolnshire links, fled to the Netherlands from Boston Lincolnshire and then in 1620, sailed onto America. They joined the Mayflower ship and became known as the Pilgrim Fathers.

We can also thank Luther for the tradition of the chorale, the congregational singing which we can hear in the many churches of Norfolk. The volume of churches does not sadly correspond to the size of congregations but when I raised this with a church historian, he replied that the Hansa centuries certainly could not fill the churches.

It was something I became accustomed to as I started to follow the Hanseatic routes. Merchants traded their souls by pouring money into wonderful Gothic cathedrals and churches which populations could not possibly live up to.

But those churches and congregations, encouraged by Luther, inspired music over centuries including Bach (1685–1750), Beethoven (1770–1827), and Brahms (1833–1897).

Kit particularly loved the Brahms German Requiem for its humanity and forgiveness. I reckon that the tender reconciliation of violin and cello in Brahms' Andante section of the Double Concerto, which followed his falling out with his violinist friend, Joachim, could resolve almost any feud. I think of the photograph on the cover of this book, taken of Kit in his twenties, at Aldeburgh. It was artful at the time but now looks between worlds, music from the North Sea. I guess he would have been playing Brahms.

I have found, perhaps by being open to grief, that I have come to appreciate the German soul, so far as music is concerned. German folk music too has bled into the music of the Austrian Jewish Mahler (1860–1911) who is not Hanseatic but whose music tells us about life and death so belongs on this journey.

Because I travel up the Baltic states to Finland, I am also staking Sibelius for my musical epiphany. There is a harmonic idiom identified in the 13th century Worcester Cathedral fragments of musicology which is claimed as English/Scandinavian. The Hanseatic route can be called musical and spiritual as well as mercantile.

The former director of the British Museum, Sir Neil MacGregor, in his book, *Germany Memories of a Nation*, devotes a chapter to the Hansa on the grounds of its extraordinary German led commercial network.

MacGregor quotes Cornelia Linde, of the German Historical Institute:

"The Hansa was a very strange beast in that it had no officials, no seal, no statues, no army, no navy, no ships. Those were all individually owned by the merchants. It was very much based on an economy of trust. One element that bound most of the Hansa merchants together was the language they spoke, Low German. Another was family ties. so usually somebody in Lubeck would know exactly who they were dealing with in Riga and the chances are they might be in some way related."

The great achievement of this commercial and cultural network was its linking of eastern and western Europe. It took Margaret Thatcher and Ronald Reagan in the 1980s to celebrate a wider and more dynamic post-war Europe, with the dissolution of the Soviet Union and the reunification of Germany. I remember, as a visiting journalist, watching Mrs Thatcher's bracing speech on freedom given in Warsaw in November 1988.

She said: "You will find in Britain and Europe a great readiness for more contacts of every sort, together with a wish to see the peoples of eastern Europe play a much fuller part in the life of Europe as a whole, and that is why we are keen to expand the economic and trade links between the countries of the European community and of eastern Europe; that is why we welcome the bold and courageous reforms being undertaken by President Gorbachev in the Soviet Union and earnestly hope that will succeed."

The Berlin Wall fell a year later in 1989. Poland became a member of NATO as part of the Warsaw Pact in 1999. It joined the EU in 2004. Gorbachev's reforms made him a hero in the west but created the unforgiving conditions for President Putin, who regarded the eastern spread of NATO as a threat and a humiliation.

Prime Minister Thatcher's rather Hanseatic vision of a commercial network linking western and eastern Europe was realised but alas, it has not brought peace with it.

Only connect. The new Hansa, set up in the late 20th century as a civilian endeavour with links to institutions such as the Council of Europe is a cultural rather than a trading alliance but the shared history is the bond. You could describe it as another form of European Union but with a natural NATO based bulwark against the power of Russia.

It feels bracing, those North Sea and Baltic winds and fighting for democracy rather than taking it for granted.

Since the Russian invasion of Ukraine, the UK has rediscovered its relationship with the Baltic, supporting those clear, bright, democratic countries which look to NATO and to Europe.

I see NATO on my doorstep in Norfolk as the F35 planes circle round Marham airbase a mile from my home. Ukrainian soldiers are being trained nearby at Thetford, on Ministry of Defence land.

King Charles was to have made his first official visit to France but because of some civil disorder there, he switched to Germany and with his family connection and ability to speak the language and shared green sensibilities it felt an easy alliance.

He was at home in Hamburg. In the Hanseatic centuries, stretching from the 13th up until the 17th century, Hamburg was known as the brewery, Lubeck was the trading chamber while King's Lynn was the warehouse of the Wash.

But I associate Hamburg with the Elbphilharmonie concert hall which I went to see open in 2017, a fabulously dramatic wave structure, over budget and five years behind schedule. The Hansa merchants built cathedrals, now German ports build concert halls, both, I would suggest, for the same ends of achieving immortality.

The wave or sail like glass built upon a brick warehouse certainly speaks to a mercantile heritage. It turned the face of Europe North away from the Mediterranean to the promise of a different climate, different foods, different heritage, Vikings, fur, timber.

A lyrical book on music and northern Europe, *The Northern Silence* by Andrew Mellor, captures the glimmering of forest and water and the taciturn nature of the northern Scandinavians.

Of course, it is easy to send up this portentous light and silence.

A favourite of my brother's songs was called *Norwegians on the Underground*, set to the music of Hall of the Mountain King from Peer Gynt by Edvard Greig.(Can lyrics be typeset)

On the next occasion you/
travel the Bakerloo
put your novel down my friend and take a look around.
Bearded man with anoraks, A to Zs, haversacks,
hundreds of Norwegians on the London Underground.
Ever since the moment when
plucky Leif Erikson
paddled up the Skagerrack Reykjavik bound,
Norseman wielding battle axe, sleeping bags on their backs,
launched their terrifying attacks miles around,
now Norwegians roam in packs, woolly hats, Union Jacks,
can you please sir tell me where can Dollis Hill be found?
this is Portobello no? No, I think Pimlico,

hundreds of Norwegians on the London Underground.
Their winter ends in May and then early June starts again,
yes it can get depressing there as Henrik Ibsen found
10 to 12 their sun will rise quarter past, beddy byes
brighter and much warmer on the London Underground.
Norway didn't want to be part of the EEC
and the kroner is doing well unlike the pound
thus from Norway icy tracks they export gravlax
and hundreds of Norwegians to the London Underground.
Norway's population small very few there at all some in desperation
jump like lemmings and got drowned
some end up like Edvard Munch, off his head, out to lunch most of
them sought solace on the London Underground.
Sweden has its swinging chicks, Bergman flicks, bourbon fix, all of
those sopranos justly renowned,
rest of Scandinavia tends to be rainier even Lapland can be a merry
go round. But those nice Norwegian fjords leaves them cold, leaves them
bored no one gave a rollmop when they had King Harold crowned even
poor old Edward Grieg people call second league people say it is one tune
going round and round and round and round.
That is why there are hundreds of Norwegians on the London
Underground. Close your novel up once more, leave the train, mind the
door but don't forget Peer Gynt my friend his message is profound, envy
leads to wanderlust, that is why Norwegians must ride for all eternity the
London Underground.

The Norse sagas naturally speak to wanderlust. From western Norway to the Faroes and onto Iceland and Greenland. Leif Erikson was the son of Erik the Red who discovered and named Greenland in the 10th century. Erikson sailed further and found Newfoundland. Thorvald Erikson, Leif's brother, followed him but was fatally wounded by indigenous warriors.

In King's Lynn in Norfolk, I can feel the passage of the east coast. I can imagine in Boston looking to the German cities of Hamburg and Lubeck. In the 15th century, this felt like the geopolitical centre of gravity. But by 1699, the date set as the last time the Hansetag met, it was the Atlantic that was the future.

The Hanseatic waters felt enclosed and familiar, basins and rivers rather than open sea. By comparison, the Americas now promised new trade and opportunities. As Walt Whitman's *Song of the Exposition*, said, "...For now a better, fresher, busier sphere, a wide, untried domain awaits, demands you."

Not that the EU or indeed Brexit UK has so far accomplished much of a trade deal with the US, come to think of it.

I think of these trading routes and these relationships now when I am in King's Lynn, which describes itself as a Hanseatic city, although according to strict Hanseatic rules, it was more of a trading post.

My daughter-in-law, Anna, whose family came from Poland and Estonia, and I, look out at the Wash opening out into the North Sea and our merchant, cultural, and military ties feel as strong as ship's rope.

They reveal themselves unexpectedly. Anna has a pure voice and her mother studied at the Royal College of Music. A couple of years ago, Anna joined her choir, Cambridge Voices, who take polyphony seriously and perform at Cambridge colleges and churches. Anna anxiously hosted them at her own church in Norfolk. The vicar's wife was at first irritated by the practice of singing some pieces in the porch in order to achieve the disembodied quality of heavenly voices but she was then delighted by the nave procession and belting out Handel's Zadok the Priest.

At a time of rupture and disbelief, communal singing gave us a thread. As Jon Snow had put it, we became a body of humanity.

When Julian went missing, we feared but did not know the end. So, a small group of us met in the same Norfolk church on a hill to sing *Onward Christian Soldiers*. The vicar, Kit Chalcraft, found a prayer for serenity, attributed to Reinhold Neibuhr, 1892–1971, a Christian intellectual who confronted the threat of Soviet communism. The prayer addressed the fact that Julian was missing but not officially dead.

We simply had to wait for the truth to reveal itself. I have learned to contemplate the mystery of death and in this case, there was a double unknown. The what and the how. It took months before the facts of Julian's end were revealed but the essence was as my brother foresaw it, "the unendurable image of that extraordinary flame gradually freezing into extinction."

God grant me the serenity
To accept the things I cannot change;
Courage to change the things I can;
And wisdom to know the difference…

Anna played the wheezy organ, wearing a woolly hat. I sent a picture to Julian's friend, the actor John Malkovich, who declared it a peculiarly British doughty scene and further enquired if we actually had heating in Norfolk because he could see our breath.

For my brother's funeral, at the Actors' Church in Covent Garden, the hymn singing was like Atlantic waves crashing onto the shore. It filled the church and could be heard beyond in the square by the jugglers and shoppers. Kit's fellow choristers showed up as well as countless friends who were professional musicians. We thought about three hundred people would come but the congregation swelled to five hundred. We sung *Guide Me Oh Thy Great Redeemer*, as if we were a Welsh terrace.

When we are vexed, or disaster strikes, we can sing.

This was nationally true of Estonia as well. It broke away from Russia with a singing revolution at the end of the Cold War. The term came from an Estonian artist, Heinz Valk, to describe the spontaneous singing demonstrations at the Tallinn Song Festival Grounds in June 1988.

A human chain of two million people spread from Tallinn to Vilnius, Lithuania, in August 1989. They sung mostly national folk songs, perhaps including the 16th century Hanseatic ones which refer to Tallinn known as 'house of wax and flax' and Riga 'house of hemp and butter'. They sang for their survival and for their spirits.

When Russia invaded Ukraine in February 2022, Estonia and the other Baltic states turned west for protection from NATO and Europe. All nations felt their history. The pivotal relationship between German and Russia weighed heavily. The former Chancellor Angela Merkel and President Putin personified their nations which had been connected during life times. She was Mutte. She spoke perfect Russian to President Putin. He replied to her in fluent German. Now the relationship between the countries is severed.

The Hanseatic League route which snaked from King's Lynn to Novgorod near St Petersburg became a matter for the annual Hansa council. It was debated that summer whether Hansa towns could continue relations as a hopeful continuation of peace and prosperity.

The Baltic states were indignant and Germany came down on their side. No more Hansa activity in Russia. The route would end at Visby, in the middle of the Baltic.

The Baltic Sea was the stretch of freedom, just as it had been when the Berlin Wall went up in 1961. More than five thousand citizens of the German Democratic Republic tried to escape across the Baltic Sea but fewer than a thousand reached West Germany, Denmark or Sweden. Freedom and tyranny, the history of the Baltics.

Anna's grandmother had fled her home in Estonia when Russian soldiers broke down the door during the Second World War.

Estonia had been invaded first by the Soviet Union, then the Nazis and then finally annexed into the USSR. Anna's granny made her way to Germany where she worked as a Red Cross nurse and then to the UK. The Hanseatic route.

She talked little of her experiences, preferring to teach her daughter, Scarlett, Anna's mother, about music. Anna chose John Rutter's *Gaelic Blessing* for her grandmother's funeral, which she felt had a simplicity of a Baltic folk song. We played it again to carry Kit's coffin to the altar, watched by John Rutter in the third row.

This Hanseatic route is historic, resonant, economic, cultural and topical. The invasion of Ukraine by Russia has brought it back to life.

I have begun to understand it through personal and geographical ties. My sight lines from East Anglia are across the North Sea. In winter, I watch the pink footed geese fly in from Norway.

The geopolitical ties are also feeling stronger. I look at the latest government integrated defence review which talks of the primacy of NATO.

It reads: "The UK will continue to lead efforts in NATO to ensure the alliance retains its technological edge and industrial advantage. NATO has selected London as one of two locations for the European Headquarters of NATO's Defence Innovation Accelerator of the North Atlantic twinned with a second in Tallinn, Estonia."

It also pledges that: "The UK will make a particular contribution to northern European security. We are strengthening our NATO battlegroup in Estonia with artillery, air defence and reinforced command; in 2023, Exercise Spring Storm will show how we could scale up to a brigade if needed in a crisis. We are especially invested in the format provided by the Joint Expeditionary Force which since 2022 has had three leader level meetings and is an increasingly important vehicle for security in the High North, North Atlantic and Baltic."

The front line of NATO against Russian power lies in my daughter-in-law's homeland.

There is a photograph in *The Times* from December 2022 of Prime Minister Rishi Sunak among the Joint Expeditionary Force in Riga, Latvia.

The leaders are our new close allies: They also happen to fall into the shape of the Hanseatic League.

1. Lithuanian President Gitanas Nauseda
2. Swedish PM Ulf Kristersson
3. British PM Rishi Sunak
4. Estonian PM Kaja Kallas
5. Latvian PM Krisjanis Karins
6. Norwegian PM Jonas Gahr Store
7. Danish Deputy PM Jakob Ellemann-Jensen
8. Finnish President Sauli Ninisto

They have a collective look, European with frozen clear complexions, mostly grey-haired, suits, one button, except for Estonia, slim blonde suit that could be a gherkin, tanned boots.

The Kremlin did not want to let the Baltics go. On 1 May 2023, *The Times* ran a story from Berlin that Russia was trying to hijack environmental campaign movements around the Baltic to spread influence and turn public opinion against NATO.

Putin was horrified to witness Finland join the NATO alliance, with Sweden preparing to follow. Finland's long border with Russia became the border of NATO and the EU.

Helsinki's main square had been modelled by the German architect Carl Ludwig Engel on St Petersburg on the commission of Tsar Alexander I, the pro-Enlightenment European who defeated Napoleon and demanded Poland at the Congress of Vienna in 1814. Finland represented Russian glory.

The surge in Europeanism was given cultural expression in the Hansa embrace by the Baltic states. The Baltic states are bustling with Hanseatic fairs and markets, provincial, civic, ale based. This year, the annual festival is to be in

Torun in Poland, home of Copernicus—a festival of peace with a neighbour at war.

Paul Richards introduces me to Hamish Stewart, the commissioner for all English Hansa towns. It is a voluntary, civic role which has become consuming. Hamish Stuart sees a future of cycle routes and friendly faces. He is evangelical in the UK, plotting the spread of Hansa towns from Lynn and Boston to Bury and up to Aberdeen and Shetland, which is almost Norway.

Hamish was cast down by the fracturing of good relations which followed Brexit and believes that Hansa towns can form a chain of good will, based on trade, faith, ale and choirs. I catch on that this is a citizen led project, rather than a political one and that amateur enthusiasm gets you only so far.

This is a book about how relationships are formed; how the seismic change of Brexit followed by the Russian invasion of the Ukraine brought into relief a medieval trading route.

The political historian Michael Sturmer is quoted by Neil MacGregor.

"If you ask people from Hamburg or Bremen where their friends and neighbours are and which are their closest neighbours, they would invariably say Britain and Scandinavia."

Then you have the German airline Lufthansa, the Hansa of the air.

And it happened to be the route of friendship which linked me, writing here in Norfolk, with the roots of my daughter-in-law whose family took the Hanseatic route to settle in the UK. The 'Easterlings' of the Baltic states came to find a home in East Anglia.

I am going in search of Anna's family and their personal routes: I want to find our friends in the Baltics. I look at Anna's niece with her white gold hair and ice blue eyes and see the Hanseatic route personified.

There is another thread woven into my family fabric. Before my brother died, he had been working on a pilgrim route through Norfolk, which he hoped would rekindle interest in some neglected churches. One of them was the one he came to live in, after divorce expelled him from his family home into the vestry opposite.

He died, of severe heart disease and exhaustion, before he could accomplish his routes but Kit's Cordelia like daughter, Gus, determined to save the church after her father's death and fought to buy back the family home in Stoke Ferry.

She believed that she could run it on Kit's pilgrim route to King's Lynn. Some rooms would be called Pilgrim Rooms, others Hanseatic.

The great age of pilgrimages and the Hanseatic League coincided and a revival of both is certainly good for tourism. We can start with the route from Stoke Ferry; to the north Walsingham and King's Lynn, to the south Ely, via Kit's designated churches. It could be a river walk, or a boat, just as Kit would row his son, Rollo, along the Ouse to his cathedral school in order to make it more enticing. A pilgrimage along a river, via a lake, to a cathedral in time for Evensong. This was Kit's final idea and my task.

Kit wrote a lullaby for Gus when she was a teenager, which I read at the Christening of my granddaughter, Cressida, a few months after Kit died, a little briskly because Gus was in the front row of the church and my sister, Jojo, further back sitting with our mother, and none of us wished to cry. These are the first and last verses from it.

Alright then father, this is the deal:
Let her hear, let her smell, taste and feel,
Ten small fingers and the rest,
No abductions from crazies who have not been so blessed,
Let her not struggle too much at the start,
Spare her a hole in the heart.

Father, please let me not fail to provide,
And one last bargain, can we make?
That she's happy whatever she thinks that might take
And come the moment, which will, when we part,
Spare her the hole in my heart.

Another purpose of seeing through Kit's wishes it to try to close the hole in his heart.

The medieval age of the pilgrimage was linked to that of the Hanseatic League. The Catholicism of Walsingham was eclipsed in Lincolnshire by another faith which arrived by the trade route. The Lutheranism of northern Europe. Faith and trade.

Boston was where trade and faith met in a kind of melting pot: Luther and Lubeck.

The Reformation and Protestantism. For Neil MacGregor, musical and theological history rests on the relationship between Bach and Luther. He writes:

"Two boy choristers both products of the same Latin school: Martin Luther and Johann Sebastian Bach, perhaps the two greatest Saxons ever. In that church, week after week, the young Bach absorbed the words and rhythms of Luther's Bible until they became entirely his own. Later, he would own two complete sets of Luther's writings. Along with the many great works of literature which would not have come into being without Luther's Bible, we must also count many of the cantatas and oratorios and above all the Passions of Johann Sebastian Bach."

The resonance of choirs and momentous times strikes a note. As the King's Coronation approached, there was much talk of carriages, coronation quiches, and guest lists but I was most interested in the music, not least because John Rutter was involved.

And a couple of weeks before the event, I went to an anniversary concert for the commendable organisation the Music in Secondary Schools Trust, which aims to give children from all backgrounds the chance to play in an orchestra. It is Germanic aim.

Andrew Lloyd-Webber sponsored a programme for this and the concert was held at his theatre, Theatre Royal, Drury Lane. Afterwards, his wife, Lady Lloyd-Webber, led a group of us up back stairs and corridors and through a kitchen to reach Lord Lloyd-Webber's private apartment.

And there he played us a sneak preview of the anthem he had composed for the coronation to mark the crowning of Camilla as queen. The king had asked for joy, and so it was, based on the Psalms. Choristers and RAF trumpeters.

I was struck that Andrew had recently lost his son, Nick, also a composer, to a cruel cancer. Yet he could compose a Psalm of lasting joy. Sorrow and joy part of the same.

"Weeping may endure for a night, but joy cometh in the morning."

Luther understood that faith is personal and music is the expression of it. Bach regarded music as faith.

My grandfather was a west country chaplain and music rumbled from the Cornish chapels. I will not forget that crescendo of *Guide Me Oh Thy Great Redeemer* filling the actors' church at Covent Garden for my brother's funeral.

Apart from the spread of Lutheran theology, Hanse towns absorbed new ideas, books, languages, people, yet retained their social cohesion. Trade is a solid foundation for relationships.

My niece, Gus, has been living in King's Lynn and is a student of Clifton House, the superbly preserved Hanseatic merchant house, now owned by the historians Simon Thurley and Anna Keay. Our first pilgrimage after Kit died was along that route to King's Lynn ending up at Clifton House.

In fact, Simon and Anna live rather like Hanseatic merchants, with great oak doors opening into a cobbled courtyard, fires in all rooms, dining table laden with fare and properly laid with crystal glasses and damask napkins. My favourite of their choice of dining rooms is several floors up the narrow winding wooden stairs of the turret tower, overlooking the Wash. It was from their medieval cellar that the barrels were rolled out to ship out along the Hanseatic route.

Post Brexit, even in Boston, there is a yearning for European cultural links. And the Poles have a big presence in King's Lynn, even though some returned home as exchange rates became less favourable. At a sugar beet factory near Ely, all the signs are in Polish.

Cultural relationships have a fresh interest for me since I joined the board of the British Council, an organisation formed to promote long-term peace and prosperity through non-political alliances.

My first official trip was to Poland and to Lithuania. I chose the region because Poland is a key UK ally and the European power of the region and because Lithuania and the Baltic states are so brave about understanding the threat of Putin as a neighbour and nevertheless choosing a future with NATO and Europe.

The nuclear bases in Belarus are about thirty miles from the Lithuanian border and the populations of Vilnius and Warsaw are issued with iodine tablets.

At a round table of British Council colleagues in their thirties and forties, each had experience of grandparents in Siberia.

Lithuania was quick to endorse Sweden and Finland too as new NATO members; there was a NATO air display on the day I arrived at Vilnius airport. The conflict feels close and yet people are now cowed. It is just more history.

I meet our British Council country director, Ona, who is tall with gamine short hair, wide grey eyes and a ready laugh. I comment on her height and she shrugs that Lithuania is a country of basketball players. She says that I should see how tall her four year old son is already.

I remembered something I had read about the famous mystery of the Amber Room, a chamber of amber panels constructed in 18th century Prussia and considered a wonder of the world.

Amber was one of the treasures traded by Baltic Hanseatic merchants and the room designed for a palace in Berlin was worked on by amber masters from Danzig (Gdansk).

But in 1716, the Prussian King Frederick William I gave the room to Tsar Peter the Great in exchange for some tall soldiers. Later, the room was looted by the Nazis and taken to Konigsberg, destroyed by Allied forces in 1944.

In 1998, two teams, one German, one Lithuanian, went in search but neither unearthed it. This piece of history was a roundabout way of asking Ona if there is a reason for Lithuanians being tall. Almost every conversation is laden with the complexity of history and geography here. Today, Konigsberg is known as Kaliningrad, a sliver of Russia on the Baltic coast between Lithuania and Poland.

As I prepared for take-off on my Lot Polish airline to Vilnius, I had flicked through the flight magazine and noted the thick web of flight routes go blank over Russia. My phone flashed news that President Putin was ready to sign a deal to site nukes in Belarus following talks with President Alexander Lukashenko.

Meanwhile, tanks were making their way across Poland to Ukraine, a gift from Germany and from the UK. King Charles laid a wreath at Hamburg, a memorial to the destruction of the Second World War. Tanks, mud, bloodied bodies are photographed in our newspapers again.

One consequence of Putin's aggression is that Lithuania is now politically closer to Poland and to Germany. The Union and Commonwealth between the two countries which spanned the Hanseatic centuries of 14th to the 16th feels vivid.

Lithuania's 20th century history is still raw: independence in 1918, occupied during the Second World War by the Soviets, then the Nazis, then the Soviets again. Finally, after years of resistance, independence in 1990 as the Soviet Union dissolved.

NATO membership in 2004 and EU membership followed shortly afterwards. These ties are now felt in the handshake between me and the beautiful basketball player size Ona. We sidestep Brexit. "It is all bi-laterals now," we say.

There is also a rise in 'language nationalism'. The Baltic states do not wish to speak Russian, even among the Russian speaking populations. Latvia has decreed Russian will no longer be spoken in schools from 2024. The peace will be kept by the rules of EU accession, which bar discrimination over language.

It is the peoples who will decide. As Luther wrote in his *Open Letter on Translation* in 1530:

"You don't ask Latin literature how to speak German, you ask the mother at home, the children in the street, the common man in the market—look at how THEY speak, and translate accordingly. Then they will understand it, and they will see you are speaking German to them."

Ukraine is fighting for an idea of itself as well as territory. When the Polish Pope John Paul II was asked by a foreign child where Poland was, he put his hand on her heart and said: "Poland is here." The concept of Europe is stronger than it has ever been.

NATO is the umbilical cord. Written above a municipal building in Vilnius are the words: "Putin, the Hague is waiting for you."

At dinner with the British ambassador's residence in the woods on the outskirts of Vilnius, we talked of birch water, drilled from the bark of forest trees, and we served English sparkling wine. The trade these days is more likely to be services but the personal diplomacy is strong.

The dinner guests, from civic institutions, universities, media, NGOs, asked me about Norfolk and the Hanseatic city of King's Lynn. They wanted to know about the monastic ruins at the bottom of the garden. We are back in the 14th century.

Since the British Prime Minister repaired some of the damage to relations on the island of Ireland, inflicted by Brexit, there has been a softening of relations between the UK and the EU but not so far as singing goes.

John Rutter, who is guiding the music of the King's Coronation, wrote a diary in the Spectator (where, as an aside, he mentioned my brother's disciplined training as a chorister and hoped there was place in heaven for someone who could raise a smile in a troubled world) and the idiotic decision by the BBC to try to disband the BBC Singers.

I responded to him that surely choirs are the great connectors of the human heart and should they not be greater ambassadors for the UK?

He replies:

"On choirs as ambassadors for Britain: they're doing it in various ways, but, for touring, the cathedral and collegiate choirs tend to favour America (big, rich and fond of British choirs) which is outside the British Council's target area."

"The professional adult choirs like The Sixteen, the Monteverdi Choir, Tenebrae, etc., earned a good bit of their livelihood touring continental Europe where they have always had a substantial and appreciative following. That pretty much came to an end with Brexit: the bureaucratic obstacles and cost of procuring the visas have made it simply too complicated and not worth doing."

"As you doubtlessly know, Brexit has been an unmitigated disaster for the UK musical profession because there isn't enough work for musicians in the UK and since EU accession in 1973, they depended heavily on an obstacle free European touring to make up a living. Many are now struggling or have simply left the profession. We are all hoping that common sense will prevail and there will be a reciprocal UK-EU easing of work restriction for musicians."

This book is about ties, political, historical and personal, and it is about the power of singing.

And the ease with which we have strengthened those ties with the Baltic is down to a medieval trade route.

The academic Michael North writes in his scholarly work, *The Baltic: A History* "The Hanseatic League, originally an ad-hoc association of travelling merchants, had, since the 13th century developed into a mighty alliance of cities, which for about three hundred years largely controlled trade, shipping and politics in the North Sea and Baltic region."

Once you start to see geography through Hanseatic eyes, it has a trade logic. The North Sea coast has its own identity and King's Lynn in Norfolk and Boston in Lincolnshire rebalance the over mighty Midlands and the South.

The comfortable London classes looked for second homes in the South of France, or Tuscany, or Puglia, or Greece. My heart is now in northern Europe, with medieval trade routes and the Baltic crusade of 1390 sailing from Boston to assist the Teutonic Knights with an invasion of Lithuania, following its union with Poland.

The author Dr Dirk Meier in his book, *Seafarers, Merchants and Pirates in the Middle Ages*, reminds us of some geological history since England was separated from the continent of Europe seven thousand years ago by a flooding of the flat plains as the sea temperature rose.

"Since that time, however, the coastlines have undergone further great changes, chiefly along the southern coast of the North Sea. Along the edge of this shallow sea, extensive sea marshes and mud flats have formed, criss-crossed by creeks and channels and to seaward constantly shifting sandbanks and sandbars. Until the building of dykes from the High Middle Ages onwards, the marshes were regularly flooded at exceptionally high tides."

It is in our East Anglian psyche that the land is sinking back into the water and our routes might as well be by boat. It is why I have become fixed on the idea of Kit's pilgrimage to Ely taking place on the river Ouse. Somehow, in his last year, Kit dragged a decrepit unmoored rowing boat into his lake and which now rots on the bankside. We are filling it with his favourite flowers, particularly cornus sanguinea, wild roses, and lilies. I observe his strict aesthetic that flowers are only allowed to be white.

Six hundred or so years after the Hanseatic League sailed back and forth across the North Sea and the Baltic, there is still a lively population of Poles and Lithuanians in Boston, despite the best efforts of Brexit.

And Boston is brushing up its Hanseatic trading credentials, particularly following the discovery of a 14th century Hanseatic seal in 2002, belonging to a German merchant named Heinrich Knieval.

In the magnificent parish church, yearning to be a Minster, St Botolphs, lies a marble tombstone belonging to Wessel de Smalenburg, a German merchant from Munster.

The drive from my home in Marham to Boston takes just over an hour, along single roads, flat lands and church steeples. A sign says: 'Welcome to South Holland'. This is picker country, daffodils, potatoes, cabbages, turnips. The root vegetable diet was much recommended by the Suffolk based environment secretary when we hit a weather/Brexit related supply chain hitch on tomatoes and lettuce. It seemed another shift away from Mediterranean alliances.

This is a lorry route and road side buildings look like truck stops. The commercial signs all have extra-large writing: 'Fireworks4Sale', 'Buy cars and vans', 'Vegetables here'. And in the distance there are some of the finest medieval Walpole churches in the country. Commerce and faith.

There are smaller signs to RAF Holbeach near the salt marsh where RAF and NATO aircraft can practice dropping bombs and weapon training.

Military training and bird life are joint features of the Norfolk coast and they do not always co-exist. In 2014, four US servicemen were killed when a flock of geese smashed the windscreen of their helicopter near Cley.

King's Lynn proclaims itself a Hanseatic town but Boston hasn't quite got the council on side yet. It certainly has Hanseatic features—a market place, although moved from the original one, a fine church built by God fearing merchants, a dock, some warehousing, although sadly the most promising row lies under a housing estate. Then there are the names: the pilgrim hospital, pilgrim lanes, even pilgrim lorries. Blackfriars, Greyfriars, Whitefriars. Trade and God, the double-edged sword of the Hanseatic League.

A few minutes beyond the hospital, is an elegant house, with show standard gardens and past a portly chocolate Labrador, I meet the other owner, Alison Fairman, Hanseatic champion of Boston, printer of leaflets, maker of banners, broken hearted by Brexit.

Alison is an old style doer and giver on which local communities are forged. She has a strong handsome face and the figure of an active gardener; she has shoulder length dark hair streaked with grey and wears pearls over sweater and trousers.

She holds up for me her Boston Hansa Group banner, crimson and gold, and supported, with great practicality, by a sort of curtain pole. I take a phone picture and later send it to our daughter who is organising a drag/comedy night in South London. I write under the picture: "We all have our tribes, and this is mine."

It was Boston's tricky relationship with East Europe which led Alison and her affable husband, Martin, to the Hanse. Both of them travelled, Alison from RAF stock. Her father was the last pilot to win the London/Christchurch air race in 1953. On the wall, is a painting of an RAF bomber in cloud.

Alison's work for the Citizens Advice Bureau led her to uncover Portuguese then Rumanian gangmasters running local pickers.

"Boston has lots of these nice Victorian terraces and people found themselves living next door to crowded multiple houses of mostly young men. They called it hot bedding. Those on night shifts would hand on their beds."

Alison set about regulating licences to work but locals still baulked at the numbers. According to the 2011 census, Boston had the highest population of Eastern European residents in the UK.

Poland is spoken as a second language (while still a very small percentage of 2.4 per cent). Back to the 14th century, in fact.

Following EU accession, countries from around 2004 applications for National Insurance numbers, doubled from about five thousand to ten thousand in a year. There was suddenly a waiting list of ninety-four foreign children trying to get into the primary school. Education is an emotive subject in this part of Norfolk where they still have grammar schools.

Alison volunteers to tend the flower beds in park, as well as working on her own garden. She says to her fellow volunteers that they need to find a way of engaging with the small minority of East Europeans who like to swig from a bottle and high decibel chat: "I say just say hello, that's all, I say there is nothing to be afraid of."

"The Labour minister came here, the one with the brother who led the Labour party, David and Ed, I explained it all to him."

David Miliband went on to head the International Rescue Committee and David Cameron came into power in 2010 with a coalition government. In 2016, Cameron held a referendum on whether the UK should remain in the EU. Boston was the most Eurosceptic town in Britain with 75 per cent of the voters choosing to leave the EU.

Meanwhile, in 2016, Alison and her husband were taking local children to Bergen, Norway, and the following year to Rostock in Germany.

"They stayed on tall ships! We had two scouts in charge. It was a jolly old experience."

Crowning the youthful Hanseatic experience was the big dig in 2019 which uncovered the seal. Since Covid, the couple are really throwing themselves into it with Hanse days, flag parades, Hansetag conferences. I promise to come back for the Hanse fair at the end of May.

Alison emails me: "So kind of you to brave the Brexit Capital. We will get there in the end."

In the meantime, I head for the Hanseatic capital, Lubeck.

Hamburg and Lubeck: March

The last time I was in Hamburg, it was for the 2017 opening of their concert hall, the Elbphilharmonie. Before the evening concert there, I wandered through the city and found another excellent central concert hall, the Laeiszhalle. I was prone to concert envy because I had been championing the cause of a new concert hall at the Barbican in London which would have been, among other things, a welcome home for our most famous conductor, Simon Rattle.

I was editor of the *London Evening Standard* at the time, and there was a sympathetic chancellor of the Exchequer for the cause, who was George Osborne. But the mood changed after Brexit and the idea was suddenly thought to be extravagant and elite, a hubristic gesture by an arrogant capital city.

Meanwhile, the classical music world flocked to Hamburg to look at the eight hundred and fifty million dollar glass concert hall, set on a great brick warehouse on the harbour. Angela Merkel, Mutte, was there on the opening night. Later, Simon Rattle, returned to Germany.

I last saw him at the Barbican conducting the London Symphony Orchestra, playing Mahler's *Seventh Symphony*, an epic full orchestra performance. Harps, six double basses, full brass, cymbals. He added to the evening an extra performance. He had invited the BBC Singers, facing the axe from the BBC to perform the *Figure Humaine* by Poulenc, a defiant choral work written for the liberation of Paris in 1945.

It ends with a cry of liberty, "And through the power of one word/I recommence my life/I was born to know you/To give a name to you/Liberty."

Sir Simon Rattle, his back to the audience, with his white curls against black mandarin jacket stretched over his shoulders, let the eloquence of the work speak for forces of civilisation, but before that, he added his own appeal in a speech to the audience.

"We are in a fight and we need to ensure that classical music remains part of the beating heart of our country, of our country and our culture."

He would not have had to make that speech in Germany where Luther and Bach ensured a tradition of choral singing, heard across Hansa towns.

Germany did not have such a concentration of power, partly because of its history. As Neil MacGregor notes in his book *Germany: Memories of a Nation*, Germany's history is one of states rather than a nation.

"Politically, Germany has long been the epitome of loose association and variable geometry. For nearly a thousand years, the Holy Roman Empire of the German nation held together peoples and states of different dialects laws and religions. The Hansa was a flexible and outstandingly successful trading association, or free trade area. Memories of both are still alive and are talked about as models for Europe today."

It is the Hanseatic history which speaks to ports, civic buildings, concert halls, built on the wealth of merchants. If I really want to understand the Hanseatic League, I need to find its natural centre in Lubeck.

There is a provincial pride in Germany which is now trying to reassert itself in the UK after the hegemony of London. Lubeck stands for the pride of a merchant middle class, Hansa values, embodied in the novel by Thomas Mann, *Buddenbrooks*, set much later, in the 19th century.

Thomas Mann who came from Lubeck, wrote of a family for whom: "Business is really a fine, gratifying calling, respectable, satisfying, industrious, comfortable."

It is an autobiographical novel, including the characters of two brothers with uncomfortably artistic inclinations, from the maternal side. Would modernism threaten the bourgeois values of this merchant class?

Each day, Thomas Buddenbrook would read his newspaper to keep track of "customs, rates, construction, railways, posts, almonry—all this as well as his own business occupied him." There is exhilarating chatter about routes to Riga, and a discussion of "a new connection between the North Sea and the Baltic."

You can see the Mann house in Lubeck, Buddenbrookhaus elegant white Rococo front with full length windows and the motto: 'The Lord Will Provide' above the front door. But it is just the façade. There is a photograph of Thomas Mann and his wife, Katja, standing outside the shell of the house in 1953. The rest had been destroyed by Allied bombs. It is the story of many German cities and the nation does not flinch from confronting its history.

Lubeck is a city of Gothic copper green spires, waterside buildings, stepped gables and post-war pre-fab buildings. It is full of cathedrals, imagine the centuries to build then to restore all over again after the war. Its centre is a market square and a city hall which was built by Hanseatic merchants and remains the centre of Hanseatic activity.

In Michael North's history, he quotes from Germania (1458) by the future Pope Pius II:

"Among all the cities, Lubeck stands out, because it is dotted with beautiful buildings and richly ornamented churches. The authority of the city is such that with a single nod it can install or depose the rulers of the mighty kingdoms of Denmark, Sweden and Norway."

It is quite a claim to prevail over the warring sea power Scandinavian nations. But the founding of Lubeck (1143–1159) provided German traders with a headquarters which challenged the Swedish Gotland peninsula, with its prime position in the middle of the Baltic. Lubeck showed itself to be good at administration and the design of boats and formed strong and direct links with Novgorod in Russian and the White Sea beyond.

The pride of the city was a carvel type ship, the Eagle of Lubeck, a 16th century vessel converted from warship to trading boat. In 1581, it took timber to Lisbon and returned with sixteen hundred barrels of salt but sprang a leak and had to return to port.

It was the kind of thing which centuries later would vex the Buddenbrooks.

Lubeck made other advances in ship building. In 1618, a new kind of narrow-hulled boat called the Fleute was launched and by the 17th century, Hanseatic ship building was strong enough to find more adventurous routes.

The routes spun into to new possibilities. From Novgorod, there were connections to the silk road. Silks and spices came from Orient through Russia. In return, German merchants sent wool, herring, salt, grain iron. There do not seem to be records of revenues. It is pure market trading. All shared the same rights.

The Hanseatic route produced its own distinctive red brick architecture which originated in Danish monasteries, because of the shortage of sandstone and limestone and became the brick Gothic style of Hansa ports. Hanseatic cities have a bourgeois air of orderly good fortune. The ships came in. They are places of brotherhoods, civic centres, market squares, and, always, cathedrals.

The streets are recognisable from Buddenbrooks but also familiar to me. I send a phone picture to my niece, Gus, and she spots immediately that it looks like the centre of King's Lynn.

The South Gate into the old centre of King's Lynn is not as grand as Lubeck's Holsten Gate, and it does not have Lubeck's UNESCO World Heritage status as the cradle of the Hanseatic League.

Lubeck claims the solidity of the ages, in the portly brick towers of the 15th century, looking beyond to the salt warehouses. The trade routes were waterways. In 1398, the Stecknitz Canal linked Lubeck with Lauenberg on the Elbe, linking the North Sea to the Baltic.

Yet, while Lubeck became the 'Queen of the Hanseatic League' in the 14th century, Lynn was also regarded as England's most important port. It too has grand merchant houses looking out at the Wash.

Paul North lists the exchange of goods on these trade routes: "Prussian Hanseatic cities provided the grain, The Teutonic Order had a monopoly on the amber trade exporting to Lubeck and Bruges to make rosaries."

"In the western part of the Baltic, Sweden exported iron, copper, butter and cowhides, while Denmark had a bigger trade exporting horses, oxen and butter.

Norway Denmark and the Dutch herring fishers. England imported Rhine wine, metals, dyes, and exported wool and textiles."

Thanks to the treaty of Utrecht in 1474, Hanseatic Trade in the England prospered for longer into the 16th century. Hanse House in Lynn dates from this period. But everyone lost out to the Americas in the 17th century. The golden age of European commerce was on the wane.

This makes the cultural renaissance of the past decades all the more striking. In 2006, King's Lynn became the UK's first member of the Hanse, the network of towns across Europe which had belonged to the Hanseatic League. Lubeck is back at the centre of this new Hanse; it is like a renewal of vows after dropping them for a couple of centuries.

And while the trade routes across the world might make the North Sea and the Baltic look a little parochial, the neighbourliness founded on trade history feels warm. I like the notion of ale and wool and cathedrals and cycle routes. I mean to tell Hamish Stewart that I am all in for the East of England Hanseatic route.

Meanwhile, I reached Lubeck by train from Hamburg, on a spring day in March, but with a brisk Baltic wind. Even the train station seems to face north. Close to what was once the Soviet occupation zone, later a connecting station between Hamburg and Scandinavia. It may be geographically diminished by the building of the spectacular Great Belt Bridge in Denmark in 1990s but along with Hamburg and Bremen, it has the residual dignity of being the medieval city states in Europe.

At the centre of Lubeck is the town hall, dating from the 13th century, a Gothic building resonant with pride and prosperity. The Rococo style audience hall is decorated with ten paintings by the Italian artist Stefano Torelli embodying the virtues of good government. These include vigilance, diligence, unity, wisdom, freedom, mercy, justice, caution, moderation, and discretion. The virtues are portrayed by women, except for discretion.

The Buddenbrooks would immediately recognise and applaud these virtues for they are the qualities of the bourgeoisie.

But the centrepiece of the Audience Hall, which was used as a court room, is the depiction of the Solomonic Judgement. The inscription says: "A judge should hear both parties and then issue a judgement." Judgements should be weighed and considered, and the Hansa naturally use scales.

Along the gallery of the town hall are the portraits of previous mayors, more than two hundred from Holbein style faces to present day. The role of the mayor of Lubeck is substantial, for the Hansa values local government. Lubeck law was a town charter which spread during the 13th century, permitting freedom of business transactions. The present mayor, Jan Lindenau, has left a greeting for me. Lubeck to Lynn.

Walking along the river in Lubeck, I am struck by elegance of prosperity. Rows of Buddenbrook style houses looking across to the warehouses—the source of wealth. And mindful of the price of souls for residential streets are dwarfed by the churches and cathedrals. The Lord Shall Provide.

God and trade are closely related.

From late 12th century, knights from Lubeck set off for Lithuania and Estonia to convert pagans to Christianity. There are papal deeds from 1226 giving Lubeck status as the port of departure for Baltic crusades.

The Teutonic Knights, with their distinctive white coats and black cross, came from Lubeck and became a naval power in the Baltic Sea.

It was not all free trade. There were disputes, in the case of the UK, between the Crown, the Corporation of London and the Hanseatic merchants. In 1468, the Danish king, Christian I, captured six English ships in the Sound, the strait between Denmark and Sweden.

In 1469, the assembly in Lubeck voted a trade embargo against England. Bruges launched its own trade war against England. Trade only prevailed with the Peace of Utrecht 1474.

The assemblies of Lubeck, still a significant Hanseatic event, have a long history.

In 1518, representatives from twenty-one towns travelled to Lubeck for the hundred and twenty-fifth Hansetag.

The diary of the Danzig envoy records three weeks at sea to Travemunde and then horse and carriage, the entrance into city was accompanied by trumpeters, drummers, fiddlers, pipers.

The great Hansa portrait is of Holbein's 1532 portrait of George Gisze, a Danzig merchant trading in the Steelyard in London.

After attending mass at St Mary's Church, delegates formed a procession to the Hanseatic Hall inside Lubeck's town hall. They argued first over seating arrangements and then over menus before getting to matters of state.

In 1525, the Hansetag put the issue of the Reformation on the agenda. Some Hanseatic towns had already adopted the creed of the Reformation. Hermann Meyer, mayor of Lubeck, warns of "a dangerous new sect and teachings."

Any other business must also have considered the new trade routes.

In 1551, the English Merchant Adventurers set up a company to look for markets in China and India. In 1553, they circumvented Scandinavia to the White Sea in Russia. Meanwhile, the English Crown become more protectionist about cloth and Elizabeth I revoked Hanse privileges in 1598 and closed Steelyard.

The maritime author Dirk Meier muses on the legacy the league: "What was the foundation of Hanseatic power? We have images of fleets of cogs and carracks controlling the Baltic from great port cities like Lubeck…the Hansa also had a lasting influence on the maritime culture of the North Sea and the Baltic, not only through the infrastructure of its ports, but also in the development of maritime law. A system of law grew up governing such matters as loading restrictions, conduct of crews on board and emergencies at sea."

Book keeping is also part of trade. An entry in the trading book of Vicko von Geldersen: "Gert, the rosary maker, citizen of Lubeck, owes twenty-eight Lubeck marks for a pipe of oil, to be paid at Mid Lent (25 March 1381)."

Leading me up the grand oak staircase of the town hall, or Rathaus, through the glazed brick arches, across the black and white diamond tiled floors and looking up at the patriarchal paintings, is the slight figure of Stephanie Bischof, Hanse Manager. She pushes her pale brown and gold hair behind her ears and hooks her fingers in her jeans and she throws open the door to council chamber with its wooden panels and brick work resonant of authority, respectability, and of course, discretion.

The carvings are of the church spires and the grand town hall itself is dwarfed by St Mary's Church opposite, with its small warning sculpture of a devil outside. Protestant permission for wealth so long as always in fear of God.

In another chamber, an entire wall is taken up with the painting of a 16th century sea battle of Lubeck. Trade may be peaceful but politics is not.

Stephanie has joined a medieval trade organisation with her modern sensibilities. Hansa these days represents "people to people cooperation beyond borders," she says rather than markets of wool and timber, although markets are still central to the structure of international friendships.

The resurgence of the Hansa began in the 1980s when the Netherlands had the idea of inviting Hanseatic to celebrate their heritage.

"We are more generous on perspective," says Stefanie with her upturned smile. The Hanseatic League is deeply felt but hard to police. It was never formally founded and never formally disbanded. There were no members lists, and no records of revenues. Like friendship itself, it is hard to pin down.

You have to prove historic relations but you don't have to be certified as a Hansa city. Even Bergen was really only a post.

There are now hundred and ninety-two member towns and cities, with twenty Russian Hanseatic towns inactive. The Russians have broken the spirit of the Hanseatic League, along with razing Ukrainian cities to the ground.

Stefanie said: "Before the war started, the assembly took the decision to keep informal contacts; I used to say that the charm of the Hansa is that it is below radar of big politics, even with Brexit negotiations or Russian sanctions it still worked well, people to people."

"It was an orientation towards Hanseatic values, European values. Keeping this relationship, this used to work, but not after war."

At a meeting of the board, the decision was taken to cancel all Russian activities.

Each year, there is a Hanseatic festival, a chance for all the Hansa town delegates to meet. This year, it is in Torun Poland, birth place of Copernicus. Next year, it is Gdansk. There can be no place for Russia.

Stefanie says that the decision to suspend Russia from the league was taken with a heavy heart.

"The decision on Russia was unanimous but the generation who built this relationship for decades with Russian cities, it was close to their heart, it reminded us of the positive relationships we had even during the Iron Curtain. When one of the churches in Novgorod was completely destroyed, it was rebuilt with donations from Hanseatic cities, as an exercise in solidarity. It is an emotional topic to many people."

Perhaps the great author of Lubeck, Thomas Mann, can show by example. After the war ended in 1945, Thomas Mann gave a speech in the Library of Congress on 'Germany and the Germans'. He said the time had come to identify the 'good Germans' 'the other Germans'.

The decision will not be reviewed until the war is over and meanwhile, the Hanseatic cities in the Baltic states and Poland are calling for more help for Ukraine.

"The general line is clear. We have looked at ways of cooperation, organising transport for aid and medicine. If the application is from a Ukraine city that would be regarded very positively."

Culture may be stronger than trade now for the Hanseatic League but trade is still flourishing.

"Bi-lateral contacts happen for us, then there is culture and tourism. Hansa has an association with Council of Europe which is concerned with heritage and so open to any topics the Hanseatic cities consider important for cooperation."

My ears prick up. Heritage, you say? East Anglia recently made a bid for UNESCO with working groups on fair trade and sustainability. Cooperation on archives, artists displayed on Hanseatic days.

If there are disputes between cities, they can be peacefully resolved; Hanse towns pride themselves on good will despite national differences. It is like local politics on a grand European scale. There might never have been a need for Brexit if Boston had spent more time with Bremen.

Hansa was certified in 1991 as the cultural route of the Council of Europe, the international organisation founded in 1949 and championed by Winston Churchill to uphold human rights, democracy and the rule of law in Europe.

On the Council of Europe website, it says "the Hansa could be seen as a medieval forerunner to the European Union and thus constitutes an invaluable heritage from a common European past." It lists the Hansa countries as Germany, Latvia, Netherlands, Poland, Russian Federation, Sweden, United Kingdom, Finland, Lithuania, and Norway.

It proclaims that the hundred and ninety Hanseatic member cities share the same democratic rights and the same European values—free trade, free movement and protection of citizens. It continues: "Given the tensions within Europe today, this network represents an important means of peaceful and respectful co-existence. In addition, the Youth Hansa initiative brings together young people from the Hanseatic cities, so as to transfer these values to the next generation."

On Instagram, a meeting in Oldenzaal, Dutch and Germans, slightly geeky, in front of northern European architecture. Suits and smiles.

Youth leaders. Hanseatic day programme for founder—aged fifteen to twenty-six started in 1998. Youth Speaker Rachid Hadaoui,

Why did Hansa lose power in the 17th century? Political changes, new trading routes of America, and a shift of power from Germany to France. By the early 19th century, 1808, almost all German speaking territory from the Netherlands to the Russian frontier was under French control.

In the battle of Austerlitz, in December 1805, Napoleon defeated the Austrians and entered Vienna. In 1806, after a thousand years of existence, the Holy Roman Empire of the German nation had been dissolved. Napoleon marched through the Brandenburg Gate and entered Berlin.

No wonder Germany yearned for a fabled medieval glory. Richard Wagner would go onto to transform the sagas of the Vikings and the poetry of the German Middle Ages into his Ring Cycle. Folk lore and ale produced a nostalgia, recast as wicked propaganda.

Munich beer hall was the meeting place for Hitler's Nazi party in the 1920s. But at last, traditions of costume and food are free of recent history. And the Hansa markets and stalls are there to spread goodwill.

Stefanie says: "It is more socially purposeful now. The discussion now is historically how fair was Hansa trade. But some of the products are the same. Beer, for instance."

She also cites the principles of the Council of Europe:

"Human rights, cultural democracy, cultural diversity and identity and mutual exchange and enrichment across borders and centuries."

"It allows Intercultural dialogue and promotes knowledge and understanding of a European cultural identity."

Cooperation now is as likely to on sustainability as customs.

This common heritage is the foundation of goodwill. The common language is beer.

"The advantage of Hansa is local relevance, responding to needs of cities, though different in size they have shared heritage, natural relation to each other."

"These days when nationalist tendencies growing it is important to keep these connections independent of what political parties are doing. Cross border relations between people strengthened by shared heritage, and it feels bottom up."

It can also be a form of culinary tourism. Later that evening, my husband, Kim, and I go to a Hanseatic restaurant in Lubeck; no salted herring but we do have cod and red cabbage and beetroot. I do not underestimate the change in taste. I remember our UK Mutte, Nigella Lawson coming out for beetroot about five years ago, and what used to be a childhood punishment suddenly became high cuisine, the basis of salads, herbal drinks, chocolate brownies.

There is science behind the switch, nitric oxide from beetroot increases blood flow and so beetroot is now classed as a superfood. The cod is full of protein. The smell of cabbage may be a Proustian memory of school but it tastes different here, in this cosy restaurant looking out onto the Hanseatic Street.

If we are to embrace the new Hansa, we had better start with the food.

It also turns out that humankind adapts short-term to climate catastrophe. Rather than doubling down on 1.5 centigrade, we are looking to the Baltic as a new holiday destination now that Greece and Italy are reaching unbearable temperatures. I keep quiet about my discovery of the jewel of the Baltic, the Hanseatic city of Visby, on Sweden's Gotland peninsular.

Visby

From Lubeck, Hanseatic boats would sail onto Visby, in middle of the Baltic. This walled Hanseatic city has UNESCO world heritage status for its extraordinarily preserved medieval buildings. After Germany, it is a particular source of wonder to see buildings that have not had to be reconstructed after the Second World War.

We fly to Stockholm and then a short flight on but it feels far removed from the metropolis and its rhythm and news.

I am grateful for the distance because it is the week of sad, inevitable news that a hiker has found Julian's body and speculation has finally ceased.

I remembered Julian's interest in Vikings—he looked and sometimes behaved like one—and in ancient stones of which there are plenty in these parts. Visby is an island of iron age burial grounds, Viking harbours and hundreds of abandoned limestone medieval churches, victims of the Lutheran Reformation, just as Norfolk has the ruins of Thomas Cromwell.

Runic stones from AD 400 are illustrated with ships and oars, a race of sea farers. Explorers and then traders; exchange of goods, the foundation of the European economy.

The commercial network from the rivers to the sea created the greatest economic and political order since the Romans. In his enticing work, *Seafarers, Merchants and Pirates in the Middle Ages*, Dirk Meier cites that:

"…archaeological finds around the North Sea and Baltic prove for example that millstones of Rhineland basalt, large jars of Norwegian soapstone, iron from Sweden, quicksilver from southern Europe combs and cloths from Friesland (a Dutch province), as well as furs and slaves from the east were being traded and that in the early Middle Ages, huge numbers of Arab coins and even silk reached the Baltic region."

"Without river, coastal and high sea shipping, none of these goods would have become so widespread. In the early Middle Ages, a whole economic community evolved on the shores of the North Sea and the Baltic. From the High Seas came the Hanseatic League."

I clear my head with a walk along the pebbled beach, in the midst of this trading route, watching the evening swimmers.

We are staying on a camping site which is called an eco-lodge so can charge five star hotel prices. From our binoculars, we can look out on the virtually tideless Baltic coats duck (the world of Ibsen!) and cruise ships (more our world, I am afraid) and there is something familiar about the rough grass and pine trees.

It reminds me of the Norfolk coast and the whirring wings of swans are familiar.

Up to forty different nesting birds are in these coastal meadows. We walk along the woodland path to a Gotland harbour of wooden buildings—now more remote, more Shetland than Norfolk, and find a bakery.

Croissants in an array of spices—cinnamon, cardamom, ginger—which would have once come across from the east via Novgorod Russia, via Visby and then to Germany. I take a photograph of the flaxen hair bakery assistants and send to my daughter-in-law. "You have so many cousins."

Visby's age of great wealth was in the early centuries of the Hanseatic League as the only route to Russia. Merchants from Russia and from Germany came to Visby in the 12th century. The 13th century town wall was built to regulate trade.

The great trade age was followed by decline of the 14th century, the Black Death in 1350, and then King Valdemar Atterdag of Denmark's invasion in 1361. I am starting a Google doc of who invades whom in the Baltic over the following centuries, although I notice poor old Estonia never invades anyone.

Trade and religion were buffeted as Protestantism spread and Sweden and Denmark fought over control of Gotland. For example, The Victual Brothers, followers of deposed Swedish king, Albrekt of Mecklenburg were ousted by the Teutonic Order, in alliance with the Hanseatic League.

Sweden ruled with the Treaty of Bromsebro in 1645. The Danes returned in 1676. Later, the Gotlandic merchants in the 18th century acquired their own ships.

Once a battleground, in the last century Gotland became a refuge. During the Second World War, more than eleven thousand Baltic refugees, mostly from Estonia and Latvia, fled from the Germans to Gotland between 1943 and 1946.

In Visby's Cathedral, there is a memorial to the steamship, Hansa, sunk by a Russian submarine torpedo in 1944. Eighty-four passengers died.

Visby is one of the loveliest cities that I have ever seen, its rust-coloured stepped tile roofs surrounded by the medieval city wall. It is full of 12th to 14th century churches and towers. We follow cobbled streets with houses festooned with yellow roses up to the top of the battlements.

Here you can look down on church roofs, the fairy tale cathedral, although with distinctive Gotland towers, the Hanseatic merchant houses, the harbour beyond.

A trading route, a sea port, a link from King's Lynn to Russia.

The Hanseatic merchant houses are distinctive with layers of floors divided between storage and living space, the limestone store houses only in use during the sailing season between April and September.

Seven hundred storehouses were built in Visby in the 13th and 14th centuries. The top floor loading doors face the streets, chilled goods are stored in cellars, the showroom is the ground floor with merchants' office. I send pictures to Simon Thurley and Anna Keay to let them know they have some competition, although no turrets so far.

Then I light candles for Julian and for Kit inside the cathedral, the only medieval church to survive the Reformation and restored in the late 19th century.

As in Lubeck and Torun, it was the Hanseatic traders who built the churches. A levy on the German traders.

Michael North makes the link between the building of churches and the choral tradition of the Baltic: "The building of cathedral schools in Denmark and Norway, and later in Sweden and Finland, seems to have promoted the training of choristers with the earliest examples of notation from the Liber daticus Lundensis insisting the reworking of European melodies."

"From this time, we also find evidence of the use of organs and polyphony in religious services. …Hanseatic city registers note expenditures for musicians and organ construction."

The altar piece is 1905 and shows the Adoration of the Magi with depictions of St Nicholas, Bridget of Sweden and Saint Olaf; the decorated wooden pulpit from 1684 is a gift from a German trader. The Hanseatic route is behind so many objects.

The ghosts of trade are here in Visby. Gotlanders made metalwork ships, baptismal fonts of limestone and bred horses. In turn, they traded furs and beeswax from Novgorod, northern capital of Russia empire selling the goods on to Denmark. Meanwhile, boats would pull into the harbour with salted fish from Skane and dried fish from Norway.

Fish was particularly in demand during fasting within the Catholic church. The sale came from the salt mines of Luneburg in the north of Germany. Huge quantities of wine and beer imported from the Rhineland and German cities. Merchants in Visby also traded corn, although most of grain came from Poland.

We look out of our little wooden eco-lodge at the lashing rain and Baltic winds overnight thinking of traders in that sea.

And the following day, we bicycle along the coast back for more ruins more merchant houses more Gotland—dangers of travel.

My daughter-in-law, Anna, messages me to say that she has heard the Today programme on BBC radio 4 play out to Puccini's *mio babbino caro* in reference to *Room with a View* to mark the week that Julian's body was found.

I am overwhelmed by the poignancy of the past. So this is how lives are played out. Memento Mori.

As I explored the streets of Florence, heavily pregnant during the filming *Room with a View*, what if we had known that Julian would meet his end too early in a blizzard on a Californian mountain. How would we have behaved differently?

Henry who has talked about cracking on and ducking the public swirl of grief finally posts on Instagram. It is a picture of him aged about two in Florence with Julian. Jules is bending down so he is level with Henry, an elf-like blond figure in a raincoat.

Henry writes: "My father, my friend. An extraordinary man who never rested is finally now resting, and I know there is nowhere else he would rather be. His spiritual affinity and harmony with the mountains earned him the right to leave his soul up there. It has been beyond a privilege to attempt to tread in, and learn from, his footsteps and summits of the years. Rest well, Dad. I miss you hugely. Thank you for it all."

I sit on the little verandah with the rain falling beyond looking out at the sea and the pine wood beyond the beach and listening on earphones to a favourite hymn *How Great Thou Art*, based on the Swedish hymn *O Store Gud*, written in 1885 by Carl Boberg from Psalm 8.

He had been listening to church bells when a storm blew up and then subsided. The hymn ends with the "silent, dark edge of the pine forest." Storms and sorrow will pass.

Kit had included the hymn in an unpublished two hander chamber opera he wrote about the friendship between Freddie Mercury and Monserrat Caballe which culminated in their famous performance of Barcelona. He understood its contrasting emotional weight.

Our connecting flight from Visby is delayed so we spend a day in Stockholm. At the royal palace, I obviously head for the vaults, more interested in medieval bricks, axes, and crossbows than the baroque beauty of the staterooms. I buy a miniature knight's costume for my grandson, Billy. The polite Swede asks if I would like to try it on and I say puzzled that it is not for me.

Others head for the crown jewels but I am staring at a cabinet of fish hooks, cod, and pike bones with beads made of amber and bone. These are the brickmakers and stonemasons I have seen at Lubeck clay blocks dried before being fired into a kiln-stacked in neat piles. Ships! Monks! Knights with red crosses, merchant houses, piles of squirrel fur. These are my people.

Chapter 4
Baltic Journey

These symphonies of mine are more in the nature of professions of faith than my other works.

—Sibelius

The first night of the Proms, 2023, begins with Finlandia by Sibelius, composed in 1899. It is conducted by the Finnish-Ukrainian conductor Dalia Stasevska, so you get the contemporary reference. And to rachet up the emotion, the choir is the BBC Singers, under threat of being disbanded by the BBC. Nationalism and music hand-in-hand.

In the winter of 1939, Finland's thirty-two tanks held off the Red Army, and Sibelius's choral hymn of hope was played.

It was sung from steps of Helsinki Cathedral in 2017 celebrating hundred years of independence.

Vaughan Williams wrote in a letter to Sibelius in 1950 at start of Cold War, of the power of music to bring solace in times of upheaval:

"You have lit a candle that can never be put out."

The Proms this year is laced with Sibelius and his friend, Mahler. The Swedish Finnish mezzo soprano Jenny Carlstedt, who performed in the Proms Mahler's *Third Symphony,* said after a separate performance of Sibelius's song *North* that Mahler fought his longing for God and Sibelius fought himself, but they were united in nature.

Finlandia:
This is my song, O God of all the nations,
A song of peace for lands afar and mine.
This is my home, the country where my heart is,

Here are my hopes, my dreams, my holy shrine.
But other hearts in other lands are beating,
With hopes and dreams as true and high as mine.
My countries skies are bluer than the ocean,
And sunlight beams on clover leaf and pine,
But other lands have sunlight too, and clover,
And skies are everywhere as blue as mine.
O hear my song, thou God of all the nations,
A song of peace for their land and for mine.

As I begin my Baltic journey, from Copenhagen to Gdansk, Klaipeda, Riga, Tallin, Stockholm, and finally to Helsinki, I am aware of the taste and sounds of freedom in the sea winds and forest breezes.

The Finnish composer Kaija Saariaho, who studied at the Sibelius Academy in Helsinki, once said: "The sounds of nature, all around us, are really for me the most beautiful sounds you can hear. I feel no separation between our own breathing, the wind, the sea, the birds and some of my own music. It's for me a natural continuity."

Her music was described by the critic Rodney Milnes as 'Messianic'. Andrew Mellor writes in his book, *The Northern Silence,* that Sibelius captures the spirit of the forest. He goes on to chronicle how Scandinavia became a musical superpower:

"In 2021, individuals from Finland, Denmark or Sweden were employed as lead conductors at six of the UK's professional symphony orchestras and its only full-time salaried choir. British and American orchestras commission more music from Nordic composers than from German and Italian combined. It's in classical music that we've seen the biggest explosion of interest in Nordic artists and repertoire. From a region smaller than Texas."

It is, he says, a form of cultural Lutheranism.

Nordic writers as well as a film makers are also spreading their influence. In October 2023, Jon Fosse is awarded the Nobel prize in literature for work that the chairman of the Nobel literature committee Anders Olsson says is rooted "in the language and the nature of his Norwegian background." He matches Henrik Ibsen for literary fame. He is also in the Nordic tradition of being a former heavy drinker. Titles of his works include *Melancholia I* and *Melancholia II.*

The Wall Street Journal critic Sam Sacks describes the flow of his book *The Name* as replicating the 'phrasing of liturgical prayer'. "Something incantatory and self-annihilating—something that feels almost holy." It is Thomas Mann's mournful beauty in the isolation and the snow.

The Hanseatic League played a large part in moving Europe culturally northwards. According to Mellor :

"The legacy of the Hanseatic League and the trauma of the Thirty Years War pushed 17th century European composers north to wealthy Copenhagen, whose position at the gateway to the Baltic Sea had made it rich enough to employ the best of them."

These days, Copenhagen is striking for its Hanseatic brick and its modern Danish architecture. "So Danish," I say, looking at the block building based on Lego.

"So Danish," reads the internal hoarding by the curved brick wall and clean lines of exhibits.

Its gleeful modern design is built on a 12th century Hanseatic harbour of Zealand. This is a sea faring nation, with a natural harbour and a land border with Germany. The old fortifications dating from the 18th century war with Sweden have been replaced by a bridge. There is a shared Lutheran history, and Swedish and Danish church architecture are on display, although the church I was drawn to at the harbour was the Anglican one.

St Alban's Church was built by Princess Alexandra next to the Gefion fountain. In 17th century, only Lutheranism was permitted in Denmark but Danish born Princess Alexandra, wife of then Prince of Wales in 1864, raised funds to get the church built. Her sister, Maria Feodorovna, married Tsar Alexander III. The royal family is as entwined as the Hanseatic trade route. Denmark is the only country apart from New Zealand with two official national anthems, one royal, one civil.

The Gefion fountain is Norse drama in statue form, four mighty, panting oxen with water streaming from their nostrils, driven by the Norse goddess Gefjon. It is the story of the creation of Zealand, designed by the Danish artist Anders Bundgaard in the early 20th century and donated to Copenhagen by the Carlsberg Foundation, just as the opera house is a gift of the Maersk family. Trade, philanthropy, churches. An image of struggle and female empowerment, also Nordic.

Nearby, I watch a bride emerge into the daylight from the Lutheran church with her naval officer groom. He is in braids and beard and a guard of honour awaits with crossed swords.

Copenhagen's opera house, which dominates the harbour, is a dramatic statement of musical faith based on trade. The harbour side opera house was donated by the late Maersk McKinney Moller as a gift to the Danish people.

It looks slightly ship like with its curved front, limestone bridges and steel flat roof jutting over the water edge. The architect Henning Larsen described it with wonderful insolence it as a mausoleum for its owner.

It suggests a hubris familiar to the Norwegian playwright Henrik Ibsen in his play, *The Master Builder*.

Maersk containers are the most visible symbol of trade I can think of. I once got a ride on a British warship heading up the Suez Canal from the Red Sea and my memory is of watching a line of vessels behind me, Maersk containers packed to the sky.

Meanwhile, our vessel is waiting on the other side of the harbour, near to the small, bronze, naked and relentlessly photographed Little Mermaid.

It is sleek, described as a yacht rather than a ship and indeed has the shape of the Bremen cog, the wooden boats used by the Hanseatic League, which proved sturdier (I am glad to say) than the earlier Viking long boats.

I watch from the deck the rope pulled from the side the engines start and the distance grow from shore as we head towards the Baltic basin along the coast of Sweden, flat grey waters without wind, drizzle on deck, wind coming in twenty-two mph, starboard side Danish Island, portside Swedish coast.

The Baltic Sea is shallow and not very saline. It came from a glacier that melted and so is almost freshwater; you can find trout and some salmon here. It is a basin so the entry is narrow, but it allowed Vikings from Denmark, Sweden, and Norway to conquer, and later, for traders to bring their wares.

In his Baltic history, Michael North describes how shipping and trade and migration shaped this sea.

"…supranational structures, such as those of the Vikings and the Slavs, or the Hanseatic League, developed…there are many Baltics, which have been constantly reinvented and reconstituted by trade and cultures and by the merchants and artists who have embodied these historical trends."

"The decisive influence came from Duke Albert of Saxony in 1241 granting safe passage to merchants coming from the Baltic Sea to the North Sea. From then, this was a lively route for pilgrims and for merchants."

"The Eastland Company (Merchants of Eastland) founded in 1579 brought their goods to the Baltic region while the Muscovy company, 1555, tried to reach Russia across the White Sea."

"As with the European Union, what began as a trading alliance developed into political unions, but also tragically occupations. The notion of a Baltic League was periodically revived while there was an early 20th century push for a German Baltic region."

The Soviet occupation and annexation of the Baltic states and loss of German territories changed history and geographies. But in 1988, Bjorn Engholm, PM of the state of Schleswig-Holstein, began a debate about a 'new Hanseatic League' of cultural cooperation. What he could not foresee was the collapse of the Soviet Union and its consequences for the Baltic states.

EU enlargement since 2004 was a kind of new Hanseatic League. The EU Baltic Sea strategy of 2009 covered trade, security, and the environment to transform the Baltic region into a model of regional cooperation within the EU. The Baltic states consider themselves foremost Europeans.

The shifts from war to trade to war is the fate of the Baltics. From the Napoleonic wars to the World Wars to the Russian conflict in Ukraine. The effects of the Second World War are within living memory and part of the architecture, etched onto the faces of the citizens.

At 4 am, it is light and as the bow of the ship moves towards shape and movement, I see through binoculars Gdansk in sight. The pilot boat chugs up to guide us towards the cranes and the great Danish containers Maersk—same principle as Hanseatics.

Gdansk, renamed by Poland at the end of the Second World War, from its German name Danzig, has been the major Baltic region port since the 16th century. The great river Vistula was a route for Polish grain as it is now for supplies from Ukraine to Europe and vice versa. In the first half 2023, the amount of cargo passing through Gdansk was up by 36 per cent.

In 2022, EU subsidies paid for expansion and water depth at Gdansk so that greater oil shipments could find a berth here. You can see the oil terminals springing up in the distance.

The medieval entrance to Gdansk is from where forest oak and pine built European shipyards, castles, and churches. It is direct link to the farm drainage of East Anglia, although we do not have storks nesting on top of buildings as they do here.

Suddenly, we are close beyond the lighthouse blinking, to rows of oil tankers. The silhouettes I had perceived as giant cloaked figures become in daylight proximity, visible cranes. The sky is a dawn impressionistic haze of colour, warship greys, with pipings of dolphin, pale silk grey, and rising from the horizon a blush pink light.

Then the hard hatted, meaty armed figures at the port move, waiting to secure anchorage, and the captain is checking the boat sides and sliding ropes and buffers and we are in.

This is a city of industry and defiance. In 1939, two hundred Polish soldiers held out for seven days against three thousand Germans, warships, and planes. The battle of Westerplatte, the first battle of the German invasion of Poland, was the start of the Second World War.

The first historian of Poland, the 12th century anonymous writer Gallus Anonymous, wrote in his chronicle: "The land is so full of lakes and swamps that even castles and strongholds would not provide it with such security: so it has not yet been conquered because no army would be able to cross so many lakes and marshes."

We are societies of our climate and landscape and Hanseatic people from the wetter cattle breeding parts, were the Germanic, the Slavic, the Celts and the Balts. We in East Anglia are quite at home in marshes.

Germanic people moving into Scandinavia traded via the mouth of the river Vistula in Gdansk.

Naturally, Hanseatic history was about fish. When, during the Brexit debate, it was pointed out that the fishing industry Brexiteers were fighting for was worth less than Harrods, rational economists failed to consider the romance of our island nation.

For the east coast, from Norfolk up to Aberdeen, talk of fish can still make your pulse quicken. My Saturday visit to Swaffham market in Norfolk centres on the fish stall, which expands to game birds in winter, and between conditions for mackerel, lobsters and the effect of avian flu and townie interference on partridge and pheasant, conversation is lively. You cannot be interested in the Hanseatic League without enjoying markets.

And here in the Baltic, it is easy to imagine the Swedish Vikings coming east, developing Riga, the Finnish hunter Estonians, a place of furs. Novgorod in Russia was established by the Swedes, Finnic Slavic traders and flowed into the Hanseatic route. From Vikings to Teutonic Knights, as Swedish Vikings kings convert to Christianity. The fish becomes part of religious ritual. Christians eat fish on Fridays. God and trade.

The Reformation also integral to the Baltic story. The influence of the Wittenberg Bible in the Baltic was culturally seismic. Michael North writes: "Even before printing presses had been set up in most of the Baltic cities over the course of the Reformation, publishers and dealers from central Germany and Lubeck were using the Hanseatic trade network to publicise Luther's works and those of other reformers."

In 1524, the first Danish language Bible was published for that market in Wittenberg and the New Testament was published in Sweden in 1526 and in 1527, Gustav I made the decision to convert to Protestantism.

Luther' Small Catechism became available in Polish in the 1530s. In Scotland, followers of John Knox joined Scandinavian armies. It was at the same time that the Cistercian Abbey by my home in Norfolk was destroyed on the instruction of Thomas Cromwell. We know all about the Reformation in Norfolk, I knew much less about the convulsions across the Baltic.

In Danzig, religious riots broke out in 1523 and in 1525, the council was overthrown and replaced, although later the Protestant faith banned. There were clashes all along the Baltic coast as Teutonic orders, cathedral chapters and Hanseatic cities pursued different interests.

Religious allegiances created altering political alliances. Knights of Estonia swore allegiance to Sweden (1533–1577) Skirmishes broke out between Sweden and Denmark and Lubeck. And Russian power swelled under Ivan IV 'the terrible' (1530–1584).

History and music were foully appropriated by Hitler. He sought to wrap Nazism in Teutonic mythology, calling for the defence of Poland's Malbork castle, the world's largest Gothic brick castle, and now a UNESCO site.

It recalls Wagner's *Transformation Music* as *Parsifal* bears witness to the Holy Communion of the Knights Templar. Wagner wrote *Parsifal* as a metaphor for the crucifixion of Christ, the blood of Christ captured in the Holy Grail, a relic against evil.

But purification became an odious Nazi concept.

As Howard Goodall writes in *The Story of Music*: "Three years after *Parsifal* opened in 1885, German Chancellor Bismarck legislated to expel all Jews and Poles from the Prussian Reich: within forty years, this ultra German nationalism evolved into the cancerous ideology of Nazism."

The knights, or to give them their full name, the Order of the Teutonic Knights of St Mary's Hospital in Jerusalem, in their distinctive in white robes and a black cross have never quite recovered reputationally from their glorification by Hitler.

Alas too, German and Baltic folk music languished, although it was gloriously revived in the singing revolution in the late 1980s.

The soul of Gdansk is the great brick Gothic St Mary's Basilica, dating from the 14th century, and with Hanseatic architectural echoes of Lubeck and Flanders. Within it, suspended above the altar, from the high white vault roof, is the depiction of Jesus on the Cross, blood streaked arms, a gold crown of spikes fanning out from his head, his mother beneath with the same halo of spikes looking in expressive recognition at the skull at the foot of the Cross—memento mori.

The bright stained glass window beneath does not distract from the stark grandeur of his suffering.

I think of Isaiah 53 and of Handel's Passion. "He is despised, and rejected of men; a man of sorrows and acquainted with grief."

The pain of his mother is given full Catholic expression here too. A plaster depiction of his bloodied body in the arms of Mary—it is a Pieta of the 15th century and again her face is not stylised, it is pure grief.

As everywhere in Poland, history is vivid. The church, used in Nazi propaganda posters as an image to proclaim Danzig is German, was stormed by the Red Army in 1945, the wooden roof burned, the bells crashed to the floor. The German population mostly fled to Lubeck.

Only in 2020 was the 15th century Gothic Pietas Domini altar, stolen by German soldiers during the Second World War, restored. History feels so recent here.

It was in this church too that members of the Polish trade union Solidarity, founded in the Gdansk shipyard in 1980, sought refuge from state violence.

Solidarity's leader, Lech Walesa, is the folk hero who led the strikes and went on to liberate Poland from communist rule. For my generation, he is a giant of history and I am amazed to read on my tourist itinerary that he is coming to talk to us on our boat.

Poland felt betrayed by the Western allies over the Yalta summit after the Second World War when The United States, the United Kingdom and the Soviet Union agreed the shape and security of Germany and Europe and Stalin proceeded to install a puppet communist regime in Poland.

You can see why suspicion of Russia lingers in Poland. A windscreen banner in a car outside an elegant tall merchant house in Gdansk reads 'Fuck Putin'.

Walesa's defiance of the Polish communist state, while founded in a protest against conditions for workers in the 1970s changed the geo-politics and he was a persuasive advocate to President Clinton for expanding NATO east beyond Germany.

Lech Walesa's faith became part of his political strength.

In 1989, Pope John Paul II bowed his head at the foot of the Monument to the Fallen Shipyard Workers of 1970. Having spent an hour with the Pope, Lech Walesa said: "We are people of faith and even if these meetings had never taken place, we would have still known that the Pope supports us."

We get back to the boat hopeful but not expectant of seeing Lech Walesa. We are advised that he may or may not arrive, he may or may not sign books, his rules are his own.

Then, suddenly, he is among us, trotting down central aisle of lecture hall, hair and famous moustache now white and combed, the familiar broad face, sturdy chest and wearing beige shirt, grey trousers and deck shoes. We are braced for a quixotic mood but he is instead humorous and Delphic, speaking through a translator.

I think of the famous photograph of him in 1983 repairing electric forklifts in a shipyard workshop and that he has kept, despite his celebrity, as sense of being Everyman.

He uses this playfully to his advantage, prefixing his observations by saying that he is not as expert as his audience of wealthy tourists.

He talks of the new threats of populism and demagoguery and encourages audience questions. He is getting into his stride and says through his translator he would like some more difficult or complicated questions so that he can show in his next meeting how clever he is.

He is asked for his view on the Russian invasion of Ukraine and he says the two Superpowers of Russia and China are trying to expand and EU is trying to expand in a democratic way but it is old style and if we solve Russia, the next question will be China. It is high end geo-politics and skilfully broad brush.

What is his advice for Mr Zelensky? He says he offered him help, not with a rifle but as a Nobel prize winner, to create a solidarity of smart people but he did not think Zelensky understood, and now he is unemployed.

It is both serious and oddly light-hearted and translation is part of the charming non-engagement.

He continues that even if we conquer Russia, Russia might be reborn. The lessons of history are that empires rise and wane. The answer is for the US to 'find a group of smart politicians', then he adds with another flourish "look at Europe, the Lord gave people from France grapes and Italy architecture. He didn't give much to Poland, a short summer and poor soil, but he gave us the centre of Europe—the shortest way from Berlin to Moscow."

I am getting used to his elusive insights and jollity.

Finally, he is asked which statesmen or women he admires.

He replies slyly again that the room is full of smart people, whereas he is just a worker with eight children. If he had our education and money! How many Nobel prize winners are in the audience? The world is beautiful but we give the power to weak politicians. You have to participate!

I turn to my American neighbours, one a celebrated lawyer and his husband an academic, who has tears streaming down his face. I realise that I should not be transcribing the words of Lech Walesa as if it is a Reith Lecture, but rather enjoying his historical charisma. Here stands a great man who changed the fortunes of a nation and a class forever.

Poland may have had a chequered history with Germany, first the Teutonic Knights arriving in Prussia to spread Christianity through the Baltics along the Vistula River, ending with the Treaty of Torun in 1466, then last century the Nazi invasion of Poland in 1939, but the EU and NATO has created a strategic partnership.

I think of Chopin's final concert at London's Guildhall on November 1848, raising funds for Polish refugees and what a tribute it is to Poland that their nation's revered historical figures are a scientist, Copernicus, and a composer pianist.

After Poland joined the EU in 2004, Poles moved along the Hanseatic route to the UK, swelling the Catholic churches and, fixing the plumbing. My brother's song of outrageous double entendre, *There are no plumbers left in Poland*, was a particular hit at the time in the concert halls of London.

Plumbers to music of Chopin's Fantasie-Impromptu in c sharp minor Op 66.

I think my ballcock's on the blink from too much suction blowback
My pop-up reamer's stuck and now it simply will not go back
My diaphragm is fairly sopping
I can feel my lock-nuts popping
My head-pressure's quickly dropping
God I need a plumber—
I'm sure the clampstrap on my nipples needs a load of tightening
My whole backflow preventer's furred up and it's getting frightening
Where's the tit to my degrunger?
I have air in my expunger
And I've jammed the effing plunger
God, I need that plumber—
Oh, I've trawled the Baltic till I'm blue
Gdansk to Krakow, right on through
Kielce, Gorsov, Warsaw, Reszow
No one can supply th'address of
Somebody to rod my sump
I'm simply desp'rate for a...pump
(But there are)
No plumbers left in Poland
They're all in Willesden Green
Search high and low, there's not one plumber here to be seen
No plumbers left in Poland
They're all on RyanAir
I cannot find a single bloody plumber anywhere
They write from Doncaster to say
'Hey! I can earn a year's wages in a one single day!'
No plumbers left in Poland
God, I'm so depressed
All packed their tools and headed off out west...

There's awful problems with my male swivel-pipe connection
I'm told my cock-hole cover needs a thorough going inspection
My septic pipes are getting stack-up
I have discharge in my back-up
And I'm on the point of crack-up
I so need a plumber—
I've got this box-flange irredeemably clogged up with bushing
It's weeks now since my closet bend has made a stab at flushing
What, with effluent now brimming
And my female fittings swimming
My self-rimmer's not self-rimming
Boy I need that plumber—
Oh, I've scoured the building-yards of Lodz
I've hunted round Bygoscz, by gosh
Been searchin' Szeczin high and low
Bialystock and Wrocklaw—no!
The yellow pages end to end
I'm being driven round th's bend...
No plumbers left in Poland
Not a bleeding chance
They're posing all as Chippendales on posters in France
No plumbers left in Poland
They're driving third-hand Mercs
Talk about a fuggin spanner in the works
No plumbers left in Poland
All gone down the hole
Lord! It's enough to drive you up the pole...

We have set sail at a lick to get past the Russian enclave of Kaliningrad and reach the port of Klaipeda in Lithuania. Beyond a long forested lagoon of alder trees, birch and pine and then a wooded beach, and into another industrial harbour: more cranes, gas works, long sea wall, huge gas ships with frozen gas from the US. The war induced energy crisis is visible on the Baltic Sea.

A historically weary guide waves an arm at the reconstruction of a sailing ship commissioned after Finland signed a peace treaty with the USSR in 1944.

The influence of seafaring Scandinavians on Russia is deep. The word 'Varyag' in Russian, close to Viking, comes from the Old Icelandic term meaning 'members of a sworn brotherhood'.

The word 'Rus' has roots in the Balto Finnish term 'Ruotsi', meaning Sweden. In ancient Russia, Scandinavian merchants were known as Varangians.

A brass band is playing in the town square to raise money to build a church because theirs was destroyed during Second World War, like so much else. A little museum about Nazi occupation is a litany of civic misery. The guide gestures at the balcony where Hitler made his speech in 1939.

It was also in 1939 that Hitler made a non-aggression pact with the Soviets, the Molotov Ribbentrop pact, offering Russia control of Lithuania, Latvia, and Estonia.

Klaipeda was once a prosperous German industrial town, known as Memel, but The Eastern Front of Second World War was played out here in the autumn of 1944. The Soviet army closed in and about two million of the population fled. Klaipeda was left as ashes.

The guide was born in 1975 and describes herself as a granddaughter of Stalin, taught in school how to march, how to tie bandages, and how to speak only Russian. The churches were ruined or demolished and her mother, a Catholic, would make sure that the blinds were closed at home for any marking of Christmas or Easter. The guide's mother was a teacher and would certainly have lost her job if she had tried to visit a church.

She says phlegmatically that many intelligentsia were exiled to Siberia and when they returned, there were no jobs. Some children from Kaliningrad hid in forests and ate horse meat, adopted by Lithuanians after independence.

The Baltic states are stoical about history and climate. It can be minus twenty in Klaipeda in winter, and ferries cross to Denmark, Sweden and Germany only between May and August, a journey of about twenty hours. "We have winter, and then the rest of the year the cold," shrugs the guide.

Back on the boat, there is an evening swell but we head down the estuary to Riga, capital of Latvia, where Hanseatic faith and music are triumphant. At the town hall, we see the distinctive heraldry of the Rathaus Brother of Blackheads, named after St Maurice, a 3rd century Egyptian soldier in the Holy Roman

Empire who converted to Christianity, and one of my favourite of the Hanseatic guilds and orders of chivalry.

In the now familiar high brick Lutheran church, a serene looking man of medium height in a short sleeved shirt and wearing glasses, is introduced. He is the cathedral organist and a former chorister who has studied in Germany and Sweden. The massive Lutheran organ dominates with its dark greens and gold decoration. And the music he plays is Johann Sebastian Bach Fantasy G (1685–1750).

Riga is where I most acutely glimpse along the Hanseatic route the power of music as means of expressing suffering, freedom, hope. It is a port shaped by the German middle class and merchants and a place of choral music, an expression of its national soul, an awakening from the suffering of war.

The red and white Latvian flag is said to be formed from a soldier lying in his blood.

This city of guilds and merchant houses has on one of the roofs a statue of a cat with its tail coarsely up—commissioned by a merchant excluded from the trading fraternity.

A more soaring gesture of defiance is the Freedom Monument, the symbol of independence put up in 1931. The bronze female figure holds in upraised hands three stars symbolising the three parts of Latvia.

The lower part of the statue is made from pink granite. Its engraved message: "For the Fatherland and Freedom."

Mother Latvia faces west whence freedom came. The shackled figures face east.

The street leading to the monument has been called Hitler street, Lenin street, and is now called Freedom street. The history of the 20th century.

But it is the choral singing in Latvia which is its best expression of humanity and its festivals are the voice of independence.

The Finnish President Lauri Kristian Relander attended a festival during his visit to Latvia in 1926 and wrote:

"Seeing the great masses gathered at this festival and listening to your beautiful Latvian songs, whose origins can be traced back to the most distant antiquity, just like ours, I deeply feel that the Latvian nation has its own valuable cultural heritage and that it is filled with a strong will to live and contribute to the civilisation with its own special existence."

"I also viscerally feel how much the human race has gained with the Latvian people joined the family of sovereign nations. Both of our nations feel a genuine desire to maintain peace in the lands around the Baltic Sea. Inspired by the ardent love of the fatherland and ready to make all sacrifices to preserve their freedom and independence, our nations know no greater desire than the desire to live their own special lives, by fulfilling their tasks in the field of culture and civilisation."

"My most ardent desire is to see the friendship ties between Latvia and Finland strengthen more so that they can exist not only during the good times but can also withstand the storms."

The festival in 1938 was the most ambitious, with three hundred and eighty choirs and sixteen thousand singers. Its music and its patriotism were united.

Two years later, in June 1940, the Soviet Union imposed a blockade of the eastern Baltic Sea. Ultimatums were presented to Lithuania, then Latvia and Estonia followed within days by a military invasion.

Ninety thousand Red Army troops head for Riga. Nevertheless, the Latgale Region Song Festival was held on 15 June 1940. Red and white flowers handed out were confiscated on Soviet orders. At the end of the performance, the choirs sung three times the national anthem *God Bless Latvia*, tears streaming down their faces.

On 21 June, the commander of the Latvian border guard, General Ludvigs Bolsteins, left a suicide note. "We, Latvians, built a new, stately edifice for ourselves, our state. A foreign power wants to force us to tear it down, I cannot take part."

The return of independence came through a singing revolution. On 23 August 1989, Lithuanians, Latvians and Estonians formed a Baltic chain from Tallinn through Riga to Vilnius, and sang folk songs.

About one and a half million people took part along the six hundred and sixty km chain. The sepia photographs on display in the museum of Riga are moving for their simplicity. Women in jumpers and skirts, men in suits, school children in shorts, joining hands across tree lined roads. There is none of the self-consciousness of the social media age, and the gentle momentum, a butterfly flapping its wings, had unstoppable consequences.

It began a chain of events leading to the fall of the Berlin Wall two months later. The Baltic states won their independence two years later in 1991.

In 2023, the Latvian President Edgars Rinkevics said: "We are grateful to those Latvians who started the tradition hundred and fifty years ago. And the song is a testament to our nation, our Latvia. Our belonging. The path of awakening and statehood. With song, we have achieved freedom, with song, we have gone to war and with song, we have experienced victory."

The Latvians, once pagans, may have been ruled by Crusaders, Bishops, Traders, Swedes, Poles, Germans, Soviets but now, they sing the song banned by the Russians, *Dievs Sveti Latviju,* God Bless Destiny. It is their Finlandia.

The next port, the next destination, is the one I mind most about because it is the homeland of my daughter-in-law, Anna. Tallinn is a place of sophistication and stoicism, of destruction and resilience. Its skyline is opera houses, theatres, churches, and our guide is an athletic golden limbed young woman with pale blonde hair.

The populations of Finland and Estonia are genetically mixed and somehow the 'holy minimalism' of Estonia's greatest composer, Arvo Part, feels closer to the forests of Sibelius.

The Estonian state founded musical institutions in Tallinn and Tartu rather than go to St Petersburg. One of its first graduates, Evald Aav, (1900–1939) wrote the first Estonian Opera, *The Vikings*.

Estonia's seat of parliament was once a medieval fortress and rulers from Denmark, Sweden, and Russia took their turn here. Brothers of the Sword and Livonians followed the 13th century Danish Crusaders. Now it is a pink building called the Riigikogu for the progressive, female-friendly, tech-savvy government.

In 1990, in response to events in Berlin, Tallinn renamed the Moscow termed Victory Square as Freedom Square. It switched from Moscow time to Eastern European time. The thrust of independence takes many forms. In 2023, Ukraine changed its date for Christmas to in line with Europe to December 25 away from the Russian Orthodox Julian church calendar of January 7.

The guide waves at the brutalist communist residential buildings: "So pretty," she says dryly. By contrast, the medieval parts, including squares, churches, and cobbled streets are lovely.

Most enduringly moving is the church of St Nicholas, patron saint of merchants and sea farers, and founded in the 13th century by German merchants.

In March 1944, it was bombed by the Soviet air force, but reconstructed in 1953 to be both a museum and a concert hall.

I crossed the cool stone Nave of the Lutheran church to look at a sculpture of Wolter von Plettenberg, the Master of the Livonian Order, one of the most powerful men in the late medieval Baltic Sea region, sword ready, legs apart, a Hanseatic figure.

And the medieval warning of hubris and memento mori is close by: a memorial monument to Hans Pawels church warden—the lower part, a mural of a reclining skeleton gnawed by toads and worms.

The most famous work on the same theme is the frieze of Dance of Death at a side chapel in the church.

It is attributed to Bernt Notke, one of best known artists in northern Europe during late Middle Ages. In 1463, he painted a work on the same theme for St Marys church Lubeck, which was destroyed in 1942. The Black Death which swept across Europe in the 14th century concentrated minds on the transience of life and the futility of pomp.

The fragment of canvas in Tallinn once included up to fifty figures. A preacher in the pulpit introduces the dance, followed by death playing the bagpipes and death carrying a coffin. The text, translated from medieval (low) German, reads.

The Preacher
Good people, poor and rich,
Take a look in this mirror, the young as well as the old
And bear in mind
That no man can evade Death
When he is present, as we all can see here.
If we have many good deeds
To reflect credit on us
We shall be united with God.
We shall be rewarded for everything.
And take my advice, dear children
Don't go astray, model yourself on good examples only
For death may come quite unexpectedly.

The Emperor
Oh Death, you are a nasty figure,
You want to change the whole nature of mine.
I was rich and mighty,

My power by far surpassed that of all the others
Be he a king, a prince or a nobleman
They all had to adore me and honour me
Now you come, a frightful figure,
In order to turn me into the food for worms.

The Empress
I know, Death means me.
I have never known such terror before.
I thought he was out of his mind.
For I am young and I am the Empress after all.
I thought I wielded power
I never even guessed he was coming,
Or that anybody at all could touch me
Oh, let me live a little longer, I beg you!

Death
All your thoughts were wasted
In pursuit of the glory of the secular world
What's the use? You will become
A mote of dust at once.
So far you had the right
To command and forbid
But poor people gained nothing from it
Now, Bishop, here is my hand!

We have no inkling that death is among us until it shakes our hand but since last year, I have become much more attuned to the medieval way of looking at things. After Kit died, I asked a stone mason to carve his name and the motto Carpe Diem, or seize the day, into a piece of chalk stone from the 13th century abbey wall at the edge of my Norfolk garden. The suddenness of the deaths of Kit and Julian made me alert to the transience of life and difficulty of predicting it.

As it turned out, the chalk was not enduring and already the Latin aphorism is fading. But it is a good warning against hubris and vanity and complacency.

My role models have changed in the last year from the glory hunters to those who choose humility. I was asked by Jon Snow during the media podcast in which our conversation wandered to choristers who was my journalistic hero.

I had not really thought about it before but I said it was the gentleman journalist Lord Deedes, a former recipient of the Military Cross in Second World War, Conservative minister under the Harold Macmillan cabinet of 1962 and former editor of *the Telegraph*. By the time I met him, he had chosen to be a news reporter on the newspaper, particularly covering the subject of land mines, with his friend, Diana, Princess of Wales.

He was modest to a degree, always travelling by public transport, tireless in foreign reporting of humanitarian issues, selectively deaf when he was asked to pass judgement on politics or people. He had seen too much history to pursue any other course but peace.

The Estonians and Finns share a dry melancholy humour after about seven hundred years of occupation but our guide softens when it comes to music. While organising a group comfort break, she interjects that, "Sibelius's second symphony will change your life."

Ethnically, Estonians feel close to Finland, among the last pagans of Europe, and always looking east over their shoulders. It was the Finns who came to save Estonia after Finland's attempted neutrality with the Soviets ended in a barrage of Soviet bombs. Estonia's relationship with Europe runs deep.

Arvo Part, the great contemporary composer, wrote: "Estonian cities are basically no different from European cities. You have to remember that Estonia belonged to Germany for five centuries. The name Tallinn means Danish city, although it was Lubeck which granted it rights by 1248."

I look at my slender luminously blonde daughter-in-law and see why she would have been so fought over and why she is so fiercely independent. I also understand why she sings. Her mother, Scarlett, both studied at the Royal College of Music and worked as a music teacher in a girl's school for many years.

The first winter that my son, Henry, became serious about Anna, after they met at Edinburgh University, they introduced Scarlett and her husband, Richard, to us. We went to see a performance of The Sixteen together. Music brought us together and music saw Anna and me through the deaths of Julian and Kit.

So I was interested to read of the first song festival in Tartu in 1869 in which eight hundred singers performed and there was an audience of five thousand.

The national flag displayed at the Tartu Song Festival in 1894 was then banned by the Russians at the Tallinn Song Festival in 1896. Independence was declared in Tallinn in 1918, the same afternoon that the Germans marched in. It then fell under Soviet rule between 1934 to 1940, turning to the Germans only to be betrayed again by the Ribbentrop Molotov pact.

In his book *Stalin's War*, Sean McMeekin writes of the Moscow Pact and the German Soviet Treaty of Friendship as Stalin's great power play.

"By insisting on Soviet predominance in Finland and the Baltic states, Stalin could not only recover Russia's old Tsarist borders in the northwest but also acquire naval bases to project Soviet power further into the Baltic Sea whence came numerous stores vital to Hitler's war effort, from Swedish iron ore to Finnish nickel."

"Soviet domination of the Baltic would turn Nazi Germany into a virtual economic vassal of the USSR..."

In 1939, Molotov advised Estonian foreign minister, Karl Selter, to "yield to the wishes of the Soviet Union in order to avoid something worse."

Stalin warned Estonia that it would endure. "What happened to Poland. Where is Poland now?"

Then Russia moved to take Latvia and Lithuania. Winston Churchill proposed conceding the entire Baltic region to the Soviets as a counterweight to Germany.

Finland was of even great strategic importance with its borders so close to St Petersburg.

Nikita Krushchev said maliciously that "all we had to do was to raise our voice a little bit and the Finns would obey. If that didn't work, we would fire one shot and the Finns would put up their hands and surrender."

Instead, the Finns fought over rivers, forests and swamps in the Soviet Finnish war of 1939–1940, famously skiing across the ice to drop the Molotov cocktail—liquor bottles of gasoline kerosene and potassium chloride, used to destroy tanks.

A Finn witness reported: "The Russians have no nurses, no doctors, and no Red Cross equipment. They pour petroleum over their dead and burn them."

This also changed the course of history. Prime Minister Neville Chamberlain said in Jan 1940: "Events seem to be leading the Allies towards open hostilities with Russia."

It also partly explains why Finland was not pushed towards Russia by its invasion of Ukraine. The opposite happened. Even with its long border, it held out.

By midnight 15 June 1940, the Soviet Baltic fleet had enveloped the entire Baltic coastline between Lithuania and Latvia, sealing off the ports in case anyone tried to flee the invasion.

Estonia was singled out for abuse in Pravda because of the mentality of its "intelligentsia which preaches a loyal attitude towards England and expresses its hatred of Germany and anything German."

The Estonian President, Konstantin Pats, was taken to Gulag and died in captivity in 1956.

Out of this melancholy history is a country now known for digital innovation, for NATO forces, for women in parliament, for choral singing, and for stag tours. It seems hopeful.

We are finally in Sibelius country, navigating wooded islands and lakes in the long hours of daylight.

Some guests on the boat are disappointed that we cannot complete our voyage along the Gulf of Finland into St Peterburg, although I imagine the disruption of our holiday itinerary is not foremost in the mind of Ukrainians fighting for survival.

I am surprised by how much Helsinki reminds me of St Petersburg, with its neo-classical, somewhat military elegance. Senate square, envisioned by the German architect Carl Ludwig Engel under orders from Tsar Nicholas I is grand and lovely and during this period of the early 19th century, Finland was fairly autonomous and the cultural influence of Russia benign.

Now Finland is part of NATO's nuclear planning, hosting submarines in its waters and acquiring fighter jets, looking across not to St Petersburg but to Russia's military base of Murmansk in the north east. Finland's military hub is the town of Rovaniemi above the Arctic Circle, better known as the home of Santa Claus.

The interplay between Germany, Scandinavia, and Russia is one of landscape as well as politics.

It was captured by the so-called Skagen painters, based in Northern Denmark in the late 19th century, who experimented with the effects of light and water in the stretch where the North Sea and the Baltic met. The Finnish painter Albert

Edelfelt (1854–1905) was one who studied in Paris and St Petersburg and found his own style of Finnish Impressionism.

My favourite is his oil painting Shipbuilders, showing boys on the rock shore working on a model ship, while the sun creates a pale haze across the archipelago and in the distance, a ship crosses the mirrored water, blowing steam which becomes part of the pattern of clouds above.

Two sisters have come to our boat, one a pianist and one a violinist, in order to play Sibelius. The have a self-possession and also an intimate pleasure in each other's playing. They are Finnish so they have to play Sibelius.

Their last piece is Finlandia, that musical longing for freedom. As the boat pulls into Helsinki, with its harbour market, its cathedral, and its deep surrounding waters for NATO submarines, it feels as if we are in the heart of things. It is warm and mostly light, which only reminds people that it will soon be cold and dark.

This was part of a fabulous trading route in Hanseatic times along the Gulf of Finland, parallel to the Russian coast, then along the river Neva to Lake Ladoga, along the river Volkhov to Novgorod.

In the middle of Novgorod, the citadel and the magnificent silver and gold domed St Sophia's Cathedral, a sister to the Hagia Sophia Cathedral of Constantinople. Others went on, on to the Caspian Sea and the treasures of Russia and Iran.

The trade route has stopped short but the music remains, of faith and longing.

Andrew Mellor writes in his book *The Northern Silence*:

"Lutheran music rooted itself in the principles of penance, suffering and considered spirituality…Just as the Nordic region has proved all too ready to supplant theological Lutheranism with its economic and social equivalents, the chorale has taken on its own set of secular by largely positive values. It has come to represent the non-denominational sound of solidarity and fortitude."

For Sibelius, his Lutheran upbringing was part of his music and his being. In Sibelius, *A Composer's Life* and the *Awakening of Finland* by Glenda Goss, it is clear that the Bible, for better and for worse, is central to the composer's story.

The author writes that attention should be paid to the Bach chorales, Lutheran hymns, and organ preludes that Sibelius heard as a child; his compositions have hymn like textures.

While other composers headed to Italy, Sibelius went first to Germany and studied choral music. Sibelius claimed that he had 'read the German Psalm book back to front' and was greatly influenced by Bach.

But he was not what you could call devout and the other part of his German experience was contracting syphilis. He was attracted by Lutheranism while he also defied and defiled it.

Culturally, Sibelius was settled between Finland and Russia in a garrison town called Tavastehus by Lake Vanajavesi, in a family of Hanseatic inheritance. His relatives were aldermen, ship owners, sea farers. His love of music was his own. He wrote of his love of the violin:

"When I play on it, I am filled with a strange feeling: it is as though the insides of the music opened up to me and Haydn's sonatas with their deep serious sounds almost made it holy."

He also had a taste for Wagner, for epic stories, myths, beginning a Wagneresque opera, *The Building of the Boat*, which was a journey of the underworld and led to the story of the swan of Tuonela.

Sibelius's music, played with such feeling by the sisters, speaks of the effects of light and water but is also unearthly.

The contemporary American conductor Michael Stern is quoted by Andrew Mellor: "This is music unbounded by time, Sibelius uses deep syncopation to consciously displace our feeling of earthbound stability which means you're always reaching for something that is, in the end, unknowable. You'd think those chords at the end of the Fifth Symphony would be definitive. But they don't sound definitive to me..."

Not earthbound, beyond our understanding. Finland's glittering water and tilted axis feels the closest to me to sacred. It is the end of my Baltic journey but it doesn't feel very definitive to me.

I am left thinking of Sibelius and above all, his mystical swan in the realm of the dead, *Tuonela*. It is an epic poem in which the hero has a quest to kill the sacred swan but is instead killed by a poisoned arrow.

As it happens, Kit left behind a torn and dusty water colour he had painted of a swan on the lake at Ely in front of the cathedral. Swans were on his mind, because he also wrote a scathingly beautiful ballad, *Swansong*, about a swan dragged to its death by the junk we throw into our rivers. I am keenly aware of the swan as a symbol both of purity and death, and will return to it in the later chapter about Kit's lake.

In Norfolk, it is the Berwick swans we tend to see but I can share the joy Sibelius experienced on watching whooper swans in America in 1915:

"Today, at 10.50, I saw sixteen whooper swans. One of the greatest experiences of my life! Lord God, what beauty! They circled over me for a long time. Disappeared into the solar haze like a gleaming, silver ribbon. The call the same woodwind type as that of cranes but without tremolo. The swan call closer to the trumpet...Nature, mysticism and life's angst! The fifth symphony's finale theme..."

And it was the fifth symphony which bridged heaven and earth for Sibelius. He wrote in his diary: "It was as if God, the Father, was throwing pieces of mosaic from the edge of heaven and asking me to figure out what the pattern was."

Chapter 5
Requiems

All great music strives to surpass the borders between life and death.

—Rabbe Forsman, composer

The Latin word 'spiritus' has a connotation of breathing, and this could be the last breath which reaches the body and the soul. What happens musically after the final breath is the requiem. If cathedrals are the architectural bridge to heaven, the requiem is the transcendent music. The musician Albert Blackwell wrote:

"Just as fallen humanity is encapsulated by the image of cacophony and dissonance so music is seen as our companion in our suffering and our salvation and brings healing and harmony to the individual, community and cosmos."

The year 2023 has felt like cacophony and dissonance with corpses piling up in the battlefield of Ukraine and then, in October, the horrifying Hamas assault on a music festival in Israel, unleashing all the hell of war.

Comparisons are made with the holocaust and the founding of a homeland for Israel, described by Palestine as a day of catastrophe.

Benjamin Britten understood and musically expressed the horror; his War Requiem was completed in 1962, combining Latin Mass with the poems of Wilfred Owen from First World War.

The purity of the boy's voices singing Requiem Aeternam followed by Owen's poem *Anthem for Doomed Youth* is a heart sobbing combination of innocence and suffering.

The tolling of the bells is the sound of national mourning. I remember our Norfolk churches tolling bells for the Queen's death was what gave me a sense of communal magnitude. And I remember an opposite feeling of personal loss hearing the bell toll at the actors church in Covent Garden as my brother's coffin was carried to Charles Wesley's *Thou Wilt Keep Him in Perfect Peace.*

About suffering, Britten was never wrong.

My guide on this is a book now out of print called *Requiem, Music of Mourning and Consolation* by Alec Robertson. The inscription reads: "In loving memory of my brother, Mac Robertson, killed in action in France on 22 May 1915." Robertson, a Reithian musicologist, worked on the programme for Britten's War Requiem and understood the depth of Britten's moral horror of war.

The Times wrote of Britten's recital tour in 1945.

"Performing as a pianist in a duo with the violinist Yehudi Menuhin, Britten toured displaced persons camps across the ruins of Germany. Of their various recitals, the performance at Belsen may have been the most memorable. On that late July day, camp residents shuffled into a makeshift theatre withing the former Wehrmacht barracks."

When Menuhin and Britten finally took to the stage, both of them simply attired in shirtsleeves, the crowd could not muster the customary welcome applause or even a receptive silence.

As if by way of a small gesture of historical repair, they performed Bach alongside the music of Mendelssohn which had previously been suppressed by the Nazis.

And as they played the sound slowly worked its magic lifting the veil of torpor from the crowd. Menuhin later likened the music's effect to "the first food, the first friend, the first kind presence, the first water given to a scorched human being."

Britten dedicated his Sinfonia da Requiem: "In memory of my parents." Loss can be communal but it is personal. The great requiems capture death for all of humankind but there is almost always private tragedy at the heart.

Britten's Requiem was commissioned as a large choral work for the consecration of Coventry Cathedral, weaving Latin Mass for the dead texts with nine of Wilfred Owen's bitterly anti-war poems.

Britten wrote Owen's preface at the head of the score of the War Requiem: "My subject is War and the pity of War. The poetry is in the pity…All a poet can do is warn."

The Latin texts reveal traditional prayers for the dead of Christian church, light, peace, rest and mercy. This chant like form is in contrast to the anguish of the poet, appalled by war and full of compassion for the serving soldier.

After the boys sing the melody psalm *Te decet hymnus Deus* in Sion, their voices die away, into a tragic procession and we hear the words to Owen's *Anthem for Doomed Youth*.

What passing bells for those who die as cattle?
Only the monstrous anger of the guns.
Only the stuttering rifles' rapid rattle
Can patter out their hasty orisons.
No mockeries for them from prayers or bells
Nor any voice of mourning save the choirs
The shrill demented choirs of waling shells
And bugles calling for them from sad shires.
What candles may be held to speed them all?
Britten's Dies Irae takes place on battlefield:
Bugles snag, sadd'ning the evening air;
And bulges answer'd, sorrowful to hear.
Bugles sang, Bugles sang.
Voices of boys were by the river-side.
Sleep mother'd them; and left the twilight sad.
The shadow of the morrow weighed on men.
Bugles sang.
Voices of old despondency resigned,
Bowed by the shadow of the morrow, slept.
There is the beauty of the Agnus Dei
And the final Owen poem, At a Cavalry near the Ancre
One ever hangs where shelled roads part.
In this war He too lost a limb,
But his disciples hide apart:
And now the soldiers bear with Him.
(Agnus Dei)
Near Golgotha strolls many a priest,

And in their faces there is pride
That they were flesh marked by the Beast
By whom the gentle Christ's denied.
(Agnus Dei)
The scribes on all the people shove
And bawl allegiance to the state,
But they who love the greater love
Lay down their life: they do not hate
(Agnus Dei)
Finally, an English soldier meets his German counterpart, to the accompaniment of violins and violas.
The German baritone sings:
For by my glee might many men have laughed
And of my weeping something had been left
Which must die now. I mean the truth untold,
The pit of war, the pit war distilled.
German soldier says:
I am the enemy you killed, my friend.
I knew you in this dark; for so you frowned
Yesterday through me as you jabbed and killed.
I parried; but my hands were loath and cold.

"The soldiers sing as if in trance 'let us sleep now' the boys voices in the distance and into *In Paradisum*.

The voices of children lead the men into paradise.

Then music halts, the bells toll and the boys sing *Requiem Aeternam* and finally *Lux Perpetua Luceat Eis*."

In 2008, Kit was surfing on Constantine beach in Cornwall near the Arcadian home he built from scratch for his family, on land given to him by a patron and friend called Ursula. A fellow younger surfer asked him for a light and Kit fell into conversation with him. His name was Olaf Schmid, Oz for short and they established that they had a choral tradition in common.

Kit wrote of the encounter:

"I met Olaf (Oz) in Constantine Bay. He was loud, funny and extremely good company. On the dunes, sharing a light, we smoked and talked, discovering that we had both been Head Choristers; I at Canterbury, he at Truro. Oz told me he was now a soldier. The combination of warrior and chorister enthralled me."

Olaf was, in fact, a highly-skilled staff sergeant in the army's bomb disposal unit. A year later, in June 2009, he was posted to Helmand Province in Afghanistan, where he personally disarmed countless IEDs (Improvised Explosive Devices) saving many lives in the process.

In October 2009, shortly before he was due to come home, Oz was killed while trying to defuse yet another roadside I.E.D. He was thirty.

Kit continues:

"I had forgotten about Oz until the news of his death in action came through. It seemed to grip the public imagination. Maybe it was his job in bomb disposal. Maybe it was the news footage of his coffin being carried into Truro Cathedral. Or perhaps it was the unflinching dignity of his widow, Christina, whose unsentimental bravery was both heart-rending and inspiring."

Rather than grieving in private, Christina decided to speak out. At the funeral, she wore Oz's medals with pride and saluted the coffin. Then, to a packed congregation, she urged the government: "…to fight with Oz's spirit, dedication and integrity, day in, day out, for peace."

Later, she campaigned for troops to be better equipped and less overworked; also criticising the Ministry of Defence for the paltry size of military pensions.

In 2010, in recognition of his outstanding heroism, Olaf was awarded the George Cross, posthumously. Since its introduction in 1940, the George Cross has been considered equal in stature to the Victoria Cross.

Kit, meanwhile, was worried about his musical collaborator and dear friend, James McConnel, whose son, Freddy, had become addicted to heroin. James was consumed with worry and unable to compose. It was when Freddy went into rehab that Kit phoned James tactfully and suggested they work on a project.

"Look," he said, "I've written the libretto for a Cantata in memory of Olaf Schmid and I want you to write the music."

He described the meeting on the beach and his subsequent attention to the story, emphasising the extraordinary courage and dignity of Olaf Schmid's widow, Christina.

"Will you read it and see what you think?"

James described what happened next in an article for *The Times.*

"It was beautifully written. Powerful and desperately sad. Oz's story, but told through Christina's eyes; which was the point Kit wanted to make. For Oz, death was the end. For Christina, it was just the beginning."

"As Kit had, I found the story both moving and inspirational. Grateful for something to get my composer teeth into, I started work on it."

"I was about a third of the way through the music, when, one morning in May of 2011, Freddy didn't answer his mobile. Unusual, because normally he was glued to it and we spoke every day. We were in Norfolk but he was in London, so when he still hadn't answered by the following evening, I asked one of his friends to go round to the flat to check on him."

"The phrase 'Oh God, he's dead!' screamed down the phone by a traumatised teenager, confronted unexpectedly and horrifically with the corpse of a childhood friend, still haunts me today. Freddy had died of a heroin overdose. He was lying on a bed littered with the paraphernalia of that particular evil."

"As for the Cantata, I was struck by the sickening irony of now being fully-qualified to write Christina's music. I did try continuing with it—if only to keep busy—but I couldn't face it. One day, I shut it down, dragging it into the metaphorical 'bottom drawer' of my computer hard drive. And there it stayed, untouched, for nearly eight years."

Then, during lockdown, James began to think about it again. He began with the closing section, the Requiem Aeternam, the prayer for the dead.

And it was at the end of 2022 that I received a delighted email from Kit. James had finished the music for the Cantata. It was exactly how Kit had imagined it and his great hope now was that it could be performed.

None of us guessed how soon that would be. The *Requiem Aeternam* was performed at Kit's funeral on 2 March, the soprano parts sung by my opera singer cousin, Naomi Harvey, and her daughter, Morwenna.

It was the final piece of music at the funeral before Kit's own voice filled the church with a recording of his ballad *I Was Cabaret* as his coffin was hoisted onto the shoulders of Kit's son and of mine and of their cousins, my sister's boys.

Later in 2023, on 11 November, Armistice Day, the Cantata was performed in full at Cley Church, the atmospheric beacon of Cley marshland in north Norfolk.

I had an idea to gather at dusk, which by this time of year was 3.30, so that we might spot the pink footed geese passing by in skeins on their return from

Iceland. It would be in the spirit of Sibelius and the nature writer Nick Acheson had agreed to show us the geese.

Earlier in the week, he was becoming anxious.

He WhatsApped: "Hi, Sarah, I was in touch with my spy in Cley last night, just to get the latest news. The geese, I'm afraid, seem to have undermined us! Despite friends seeing them fly over Holt every morning, the pink feet don't seem to be flying into Cley in the late afternoon at the moment.

I'm sure I can find all sorts of lovely things to see but I can't guarantee a goose spectacle. Confounded by my flesh and feather!"

What a responsibility I had given him to provide symbolism for the day of Kit and James's Cantata. I replied that we would be content with waders and he responded:

"As long as you're not too crestfallen that the wretched ingrates have deserted us! After all, I've done for their PR."

Later he messaged: "Sodding pink feet are flying over my house now!"

I replied that I am sure we would all be satisfied with the full northern lights instead and he answered: "Ha, ha, I'm toast."

But then the next day: "Great news from Cley. The birds ARE coming into roost but just after dark. About eight thousand came in last night between 5 and 5.10."

I spotted Nick, outside the Cley centre, binoculars poised, an expression of friendly concentration. I had brought with me Gus, Kit's daughter, now nearly nine months pregnant and my own daughter, Tilly, along with friends including Caroline Roboh, who was owner of the Ely lake that Kit had loved and his dearest confidante and helpmate.

We took the path along the marsh grasses and reeds, the sky darkening and the wind chill sharpening.

These salt marshes will one day return to the sea and the bird life is also changing because of climate change. Nick pointed out the cattle egret, arriving in increasing numbers and we listened out for the chetty's warblers.

We trained our binoculars on marsh harriers hovering over the grasses. We turned up our collars and rubbed our hands and I asked Gus if she wanted to return to the warmth of the car. Then Nick spotted a dark moving streak on the distance. The geese were coming. The swarm cloud moved towards us and there over our heads the geese performed their air display, their unmistakeable cry as they flew over the coast.

We danced about a bit, pointing and laughing with delight. The geese! They came! It was as if Kit were the curating hand behind the timing because we could then wander back to the lights of the pub on the green and up the hill, the blazing glow of St Margaret's Church. The great oak door was ajar as figures, now in silhouette, let themselves in and out. The musicians assembling.

We took our pews, the church full of sound, as came the men with medals, the landed gentry, the friends, the curious, the timid. Suddenly, the church was completely full. A friend of Caroline's is a photographer called Giles Duley, who while filming in Afghanistan in 2011 stepped on an IED, losing both legs and an arm.

Giles had driven from Hastings and would stay only to deliver his appeal before driving back. It was this: whichever war zone he goes to, he is looking for love to fight rage and ignorance. We must never give up asking for peace.

Then the choir and orchestra took its place. The choir representing the soldiers, the figure of Christina, in a poppy red dress centre stage. The choir sing: "Acts of the greatest heroism, Or of the most conspicuous courage, In circumstances of extreme danger" citing the description of the George Cross for gallantry, won by Olaf Schmid.

The music becomes more menacing and louder towards the bang. Then from the back of church, the purest tones summon up *In Paradisum*, a young woman taking the treble part of the son of Christina. The role of Olaf himself is played not a person but by the cello, the most human instrument of all.

At the end of the Cantata, the choir and sopranos performing the requiem gives way to the final notes of the cello. Olaf's voice in musical form. I turn and catch James's eye which is only glistening but see rows of audiences behind him with warm tears spilling onto wintry complexions.

A soldier with many medals was in the same regiment as Olaf. General Sir Richard Dannatt, Head of the Armed Forces during Afghanistan, who had once got into hot water after he criticised our presence in Iraq in a newspaper interview with me, said he was too overwhelmed by the performance to stay on for drinks we had organised. "These things happened right in front of me," he said.

The opposite of war is peace, the end of life we hope is peace.

Jahja Ling, Associate Director, Cleveland Orchestra, is quoted in the book *Dies Irae* by Robert Chase.

"Music has played a significant role in the various rites of passages observed to sanctify this journey from life to death. For nearly two millennia, the Christian quest for eternal peace in a more perfect from of existence has been expressed in a poetic-musical structure known as the Requiem."

Olaf Schmid—Libretto

1. Prologue

CHOIR
Acts of the greatest heroism
Or of the most conspicuous courage
In circumstances of extreme danger

2. War

LAIRD
In paradisum
NARRATOR (Spoken)

On 31 October 2009, a thirty year old Cornish soldier, Staff Sergeant Olaf Schmid, was killed while trying to disarm an improvised explosive device in the Sangin region of Helmand province. He'd been in Afghanistan for five months.

Schmid, of the Royal Logistic Corps, was not a man the army could afford to lose. As an ammunition technician senior N.C.O. at Alpha Troop, he supported special forces. His record of unassuming but spectacular success saved lives time and time again. He had successfully made safe sixty-four devices in the region, and was due to come home the following day. He left behind his six-year-old stepson, Laird, and his wife, Christina.

CHRISTINA
But that is war. That's war…
They do blow you apart
Those flashbacks to the night they told us
My son's face…
Those moments hold us
Seize and stop the heart.
Yes, those first few weeks are raw.

Grief rips through families, until
Life really does stand still.
But I had made my promise to him
Swore that I would go for it.
Crying is a luxury.
His team in Helmand?
Those who knew him?
Not what they'd want to see
Nor what he'd want to show for it
He asked that I find strength to speak
And somehow raise the game
The havoc IEDs can wreak
The lives they claim
I'm far more nails than Olaf was...Our private joke...
I speak because I must harness the moment.
I'd been up to Lyneham town.
Seen the coffins passing through.
Parents, siblings, on their side
The far side of the street.
'Can you say a word as they go by?'
I promised him I would, but I added:
'Never let me stand up there, with them'.
He gripped my hand:
'Blooming will!' he said. 'Don't cry...'
You have to let them see your pride
You have to make it blazing clear
Civilian lives we're saving here.
The lives of soldiers on the ground
Stand unflinching, iron-willed
So they can see you all around
Don't forget that if I'm down
Swear you'll do that, if I'm killed
For four years, it had been us three (we'd been married two)

The only father Lairdy knew
He would call him 'Daddy Oz'
It shocked me…
No, I found it strange
How fatherhood came easily
How adaptable he was
They'd always told me men don't change…
Really? Really? He was great
Simply stepped up to the plate
We didn't argue, didn't fight
I never raised my voice or swore
Do that, you won't recover
To us, there was no right or wrong
Above all rights exists the right
To love, and be a lover
Each one made the other whole
Two halves of a single thing
One in all but name
He said, 'I'm proud that you made me
The man I am, my heart, my soul'
And I could say the same
Twee? No, it transcended that
His mates? Oh sure, they teased him
'An army boy'll be that loyal?'
He'd shrug. No sweat, it pleased him
'My sexy partner,' he would joke
'My best mate, my gorgeous wife'
And equally, to me
He too was my sexy bloke
Gorgeous husband, best mate
He, Olaf, was my life
The only certainty, you see
Lay in the uncertainty…

3. The Mother

I remained a mother
My main focus was my son
We had a dog. I'd things to do
I'd immerse myself that way
And every single night I'd say
'That's another day got through,
He can do another'
Plus, my job was widely ranged
Surrey, Sussex, Kent, and on
That's why I feel so short-changed
He left a calendar behind
To make the waiting faceable
I never ticked it.
In my mind, somewhere was the superstition
Maybe even premonition?
Time will heal, I'm told.
Not so I'm a clever girl.
I know that man was irreplaceable

CHOIR

Requiem Aeternam
Donna eis Domine
CHRISTINA and CHOIR
Exceptional, the role he served, very few men do it…
It isn't just their intellect
The skill that takes years to perfect
Above all they've the spirit,
Or the instinct of a warrior
That life must always be preserved
He and I both knew it…
He was perplexed when guys would ask

How many Taleban he'd killed
His job was saving life.
Yes, filled with that commando spirit, sure...
He'd keep morale up, wear the mask
Boundless energy, and stoic
'Come on, let's man up!' he'd joke
Outwardly heroic...
But five months working solidly
On that last day of his tour
He was weary, mentally
Spiritually, more...
Four nights on the ground, that's tough...
Two hours sleep, he'd had enough
And yes, the last time that we spoke
A few short hours before he'd die
He did cry. He did cry...
'I'm hanging out, hun. Off a cliff
Come on, babe. I'm chin-strapped
If It's been too long for me, then, hun
It's far too long for anyone
Can't you come and get me, hun?
Pick me up, I'm done.

4. Premonition

CHRISTINA and CHOIR
I knew it had happened
At once, in my gut
I never have dreams
I'm a deep sleeper, but
I woke up at seven
Fighting for breath
Aware of a visceral

Cold stench of death
They're five hours ahead,
Eleven-o-seven
That's when it happened
I thought, Oh, sweet heaven!
Behind where we are
There's this scrap of a wood
I ran out towards it
And shaking, I stood
A sharp sense of loss
That could not be explained
A need for seclusion
My energy drained
'I know that you're dead
I can feel it!' I cried
Like part of myself
In that moment had died

5. Halloween

Saturday was Halloween
I went out with my son
Trick-or-treating, we'd been together.
We'd had fun
'I guess it must be me,' I thought,
This nagging sense of dread
I went and bought Curry, wine, to celebrate
Preparing to sit up and wait
Was putting Laird to bed…

LAIRD
Mummy, don't leave me alone
I'm not sleeping on my own!

CHRISTINA

That's when I looked out and saw
Two local lads outside our door
Green berets on.
Green lids, we say

LAIRD

It's Daddy Oz! He's home!

CHRISTINA

'No way...
It isn't Daddy Oz,' I said
'Tell me that he still can talk
Tell me that he cannot walk.
But tell me he's not dead!'

NARRATOR (spoken)

She is dressed like the professional woman she is. Wearing a black coat, high heels, black stockings, an enamel poppy and her husband's commando brooch on her left shoulder, she has perfected a carapace of coping. But she admits that her days are surreal, and she feels she is in a black hole.

CHRISTINA

I can function, at a crawl I can work. That's all

NARRATOR (spoken)

Though bearing up at school, her son is inconsolable, crying in his sleep and having nightmares. She says she cannot find a way to comfort her parents, or Oz's widowed mother, and they are helpless.
SOLDIER (Warrant Officer DEANO) brings forward a brown cardboard box. CHRISTINA kneels before it.

CHRISTINA

His best mate waited hours for me
To hand it over personally
The little objects wreck you so
The Zippo I once gave him. Oh,
And dusty photos, me and Laird
Our letters to him, creased, re-read
His toothbrush, even, gathered there
With that same love, with that same care he'd shown
When he had done the same
For colleagues when their moment came
I knew the dangers they'd withstood
To get him back as best they could
I know how hard it must have been
They knew the comfort I would glean
The single thing that caught the throat?
His signature black, down-filled coat
With green tape on the holes he'd patched
From sparks of cigarettes he'd snatched
As he approached the next device
Menthol-tipped, and liquorice
He didn't care how he was dressed
That roguish look I loved best
You recognise a skin-smell, right?
I've since slept with it, every night

CHOIR

In Paradisum

NARRATOR

In the business of bomb disposal, they call the cold, courageous approach towards an explosive device 'the lonely walk'. Olaf Schmid took that walk many times. Now his wife is taking hers. More than one thousand people packed Truro

Cathedral for his funeral service, and thousands more took a break from work to line the streets.

TREBLE
In paradisum…

THOMSON
Lieutenant Colonel Robert Thomson, commanding officer of Two Rifles. While in Sangin, Schmid had already cleared the notorious Pharmacy Road, after heavy mining had cut off a company of troops who were running low. It took him eleven hours to clear five IEDs. A day later, he was dealing with thirty-one devices in twenty-four hours. He was the best. The best of the best. Better than the best of the best.

SOLDIER
I just remember when he and I almost burned down that French barrack block. And when he set off the fire sprinkler over my bunk.

SOLDIER
Once you're out, atmospherics around you, you know you're getting dicked as well. They're trying to look and see what you're doing. Your brain's always thinking about the device, how you're going to render it safe, not 'am I going to get home?'

SOLDIER
Every time we're out on the ground, we're denying them their kill. We're a high-value target. Oz never wore a body suit. It's too hot for one thing and it makes you a walking target. There's a lot of apprehension, a lot of adrenalin, but it's important to remain calm. The guys draw strength from it.

SOLDIER
He named his squad, Team Rainbow. The gay pride emblem, you know? Said that we, Zippy, Bungle, George, were the only gay IED team in Helmand. Our mascot was a duck, Corporal Quackers. All part of the coping mechanism.

SOLDIER

He loved Sangin, and no one wants to go to Sangin. It's horrible, and he loved it. Which tells you a lot about the bloke he was.

SOLDIER

It was like being hit in the stomach with a cricket bat. I found myself a quiet corner but I knew I had to tell the boys. They all knew Oz, they had to be told as quickly as possible. So, you have to man up, wipe your eyes, wash your face, break the news. There were a lot of tears. It was a difficult evening for everyone.

SOLDIER

I was in the car driving home, Stoke to Didcot, when I got the call. I hit this big roundabout, and I kept going round and round it, thinking, this can't be happening.

St AUBYN

When I was at Truro, Schmid was my senior chorister. He stood up for me against the bullies, twenty years ago. I'm a soldier now. He was protecting me once more, against the bombs. Against the bullies.

DEANO

Course, he had his wild side. Surfing in Cornwall, he loved his surfing. Remember how he used to parade around the bunk room bollock-naked except for his green lid? Six speeding tickets he picked up in France. Six...Six speeding tickets.

HEAD

Major Kier Head, commanding officer of 11 EOD, specialist bomb disposal unit. Schmid was the bravest man I ever met. He had intelligence, intuition and bravery. He was a consummate professional, a brilliant, courageous soldier at the height of his powers. An emperor amongst men.

CHRISTINA

It's now been, what, three weeks? And so
Each Saturday is harsh, you know?
The pain's too searing to withstand

We've all been kicked and beaten, and...
Blindfolded and in pitch-black
Shoved off a cliff, with no way back
You cannot verbalise the state
There's no way to approximate
Some phrase to say how we're bereft
Describe the void with which we're left
Take each day as it comes?
Oh no, You take each hour, and on you go

6. Requiem Aeternam

I held him tight
I wiped his tears
I carried him, and fought his fears
Becoming, though, his widow was
The hardest thing I did for Oz
I wasn't really so surprised
The dangers cannot be disguised
The odds decrease each time, I know
It doesn't mitigate the blow
He worked so hard
He took such pride
But he felt compromised inside
And though their task is their reward
It mustn't ever be ignored
Teenage boys
Sent out to burn
Castrated, maimed, on their return
The veterans are left to bleed
While all the rest of us proceed

There is so much moralising about the conflict. I do not want to make a political point. Oz was sick of the spin. The troops were caught in the middle. I

135

believe, and they believed, that they were there to protect our shores. That's why they go into battle. They should feel loved. Their families should feel our respect, our pride.

George Cross? That's a side-issue. Appreciation is lovely but he wouldn't have expected it. We have a duty not only to honour what he stood for, but to live lives which honour the sacrifice he made. My husband, my son's father, was a warrior. Warriors are unique: our protectors, not our destroyers. He will live on through those he saved. He will live on through me and Laird.

CHRISTINA, LAIRD, CHOIR
When someone's loved
All else above
You have to let them go with love
Sleep now, with the rest of them
Sleep well, big man. Requiem
Requiem aeternam
Donna eis domine
Et lux perpetua
She takes the jacket, strokes the ground once in farewell, and proudly walks out.
DEANO (spoken)
Sleep well, mate

We drove home through the thick fog that evening, and stood round the Aga, with mugs, Kit's friends, me, my daughter, Tilly, and husband, Kim, our hearts swollen. I busied myself making hot water bottles and then Caroline pointed out to me the familiar handwriting in ink on the bottle neck, "Warm hug, love Kit."

The author of Requiem, Alec Robertson, reminds us of their origins by introducing us to the Roman catacombs and the prayers for the dead.

"Requiem, rest, the word that was to become the leading theme of the Mass for the Dead is everywhere to be found—rest and sleep and peace."

A medieval pilgrim has written on the walls: "There is light in this darkness there is music in these tombs."

It was not until 1563 at the Council of Trent that liturgical rites were organised, with a preference for plainsong over polyphony. The processional chanting of Psalm verses would get you to the altar. The words 'rest' and 'light' are at the heart of the chant. As Robertson explains, "rest in the sense of St Augustine's words: 'Our souls are restless till they rest in thee'; a rest that is now eternal, a light that is all enlightening."

I think again of how I was drawn to the Elizabeth Bishop poem, *I am in Need of Music*, which I read at Kit's funeral, and how it in a way answered St Augustine's call for rest and peace at the end… "A spell of rest, and quiet breath, and cool heart, that sinks through fading colours deep/To the subaqueous stillness of the sea, and floats forever in a moon green pool, Held in the arms of rhythm and of sleep."

Lux aeterna luceat eis, Domine—light perpetual shine upon them, Requiem Aeternam, eternal rest, is what I think of every single day.

The liturgy goes deep but it is the awe and majesty of Beethoven's Missa Solemnis which brings it to life. The choir between worlds.

And what of the role of personal grief in informing the requiem? Palestrina's *Requiem Mass* was written in 1554, when he was thirty years old. He went on to lose two sons, two brothers, and his wife in the plague epidemics of 1572 and 1580.

Alec Robertson, with a Reithian sternness, suggests that his requiem would have benefited from his writing it after his personal tragedies.

Michael Haydn, younger brother of Joseph Haydn and said to have had the more beautiful voice as a child chorister at St Stephen's Cathedral, Vienna, composed his *Requiem Somene* for the funeral of the Archbishop of Salzburg in 1771, which was also the year that he lost his daughter.

Above all, there is Mozart's premonition of death.

In 1787, aged thirty-one, he wrote to his ill father his thoughts on death.

"As death, when we come to consider it closely, is the true goal of an existence, I have formed during the last few years such close relations with this best and truest friend of mankind, that his image is not only no longer terrifying to me, but is indeed very soothing and consoling."

"And I thank my God for graciously granting me the opportunity of learning that death is the key which unlocks to the door to our true happiness. I never lie down at night without reflecting that—young as I am—I may not live to see another day. Yet no one of all my acquaintances could say that in company I am morose or disgruntled…"

Four years later, Mozart wrote in 1791 a letter without a signature or a recipient and which is contentious as a potential forgery but which ended...

"I know from what I suffer that the hour is come. I am at the point of death: I have come to an end before having had the enjoyment of my talent, life indeed was so beautiful, my career began under such fortunate auspices: but one cannot change one's destiny No one can measure his own days, one must resign oneself, it will be as providence wills and so I finish my death song."

Yet, Mozart's wife, Constanze, did say Mozart had known he was dying as he wrote the commission of a Requiem: "it is for myself I am writing this."

It is Verdi's Requiem which gets Alec Robertson's vote as the nearest expression of heaven. "Verdi's Requiem is undoubtedly the most beautiful setting that had ever been, or ever will be, composed. The opening bars of the Introit, for muted strings, breathes the very spirit of the words *Requiem Aeternam* murmured by the chorus in a manner unapproached before. Who can forget the gentle crescendo of the cellos, to the lovely phrase expressive of the lux perpetua..."

"I would dearly love to know if Verdi had in mind Michelangelo's painting of the Last Judgement over the altar in the Sistine Chapel when he set Dies irae."

But since this book is rooted in a geographical relationship between the East of England and Germany and the Baltics, I am going to vote for the cross century early alphabet composers, Brahms, Bach, Beethoven, and Britten.

Brahms wrote Kit's favourite requiem, I understand that, because it is soaked in pity for humanity thinking less of the dead and judgement and more of those who mourn for them. It was through Brahms too that I realised the profound sorrow and comfort of the Psalms. Kit would have already known this and I want of course to tell him of my revelation. I read Debi Simons' text and translation in her book *A German Requiem* by Johannes Brahms.

The infinite pity is in both the words and music:

Blessed are those who the grief bear
For they shall comforted be
Who with tears sow
Will with joys harvest
They go forth and weep
And bear precious seeds
And come with joy

And bring their sheaves. (Psalms 126:5–6)

For all flesh is like grass

And all magnificence of mortals

Like the grasses' flowers

The grass had dried up

And the flower fallen off

So be now patient, dear brothers

Until the future of the Lord

Behold, a husbandman waits

For the precious fruit of the earth

And is patient about it until he received

The morning rain

And evening rain

But the Lord's word remains in eternity

The redeemed of the Lord will again come

And to Zion come with shouts of joy:

Eternal joy will upon their head be

And sorrow and sighing will go away have to

(Isaiah: 35.10)

And finally, the Chorus

Blessed are the dead

Who in the Lord die

From now on

Yes, the Spirit says,

That they rest from their labour

For their works follow them after

(Revelation 14:13)

Brahms said that he had humanity as a whole in mind, which is why the Requiem takes the form of a choral symphony. But he was also thinking of the death of his friend, Robert Schumann, in 1856 and of his mother in 1861.

Kit played this Requiem on a tape at an all-night vigil in his church for our dad and we played it again the following year in the same church for Kit. I will remember the flickering candles, Kit's coffin, and sitting in the choir stalls not wanting to leave him alone. Kit's son, Rollo, had arranged the vigil after the funeral and before the cremation. Luther may not have believed in purgatory but it felt like a pause as least before Kit's final journey into the furnace.

I have read since that funerals have become more perfunctory to save expense and time. You could not listen to Brahms's German Requiem without understanding the enormity of death. Kit may have followed vigils to the letter by staying through the night with our father's coffin—and indeed once performing a vigil for the family dog—but he was right that you cannot skip over the final departure.

As for Brahms, he understood that all flesh is but as grass even before personal tragedy. Brahms composed a funeral hymn when he was twenty-five and completed eleven chorale preludes in the year before his death. The final one to the words, O World, I must now leave you.

But the music of dying belonged perhaps above all to Bach, who lost seven of his thirteen children. The American Catholic novelist Julian Green wrote in his diary in 1953, how Bach's Cantata no. 32 *Liebster Jesu Mein Verlangen* appeared to him as a passage of preparation: "Impossible to express how great a part Bach has played in my life; it is he, more than any other, who has reconciled one to the idea of dying."

As with Brahms, thoughts of death came early. Bach's cantata *Gottes Zeit ist die allerbeste Zeit* (Ah, Lord, teach us to remember that we must die) was written when he was aged twenty-two.

It was one of Kit's entrepreneurial ideas to set up a high end funeral business, called Hi, End.

I hope he would have let me choose Tavener's *Song of Athene*.

Alleluia, Allelluia.

May flights of angels sing thee to thy rest.

Allelulia, Alleluia.

Remember me of Lord, when you come into your kingdom.

Allelulia, Allelulia.

Give rest O Lord to your handmaid, who has fallen asleep.

Alleluia, Alleluia…

My favourite contemporary composer after Avo Part is Errollyn Wallen, who wrote the haunting carol *Peace on Earth*. She writes in her recently published memoir: "Most of us are walking around in the company of ghosts. While it is memory that we summon every day in order to survive it is also memory that can cause the most profound emotional pain."

She took the poem by Vera Brittain, *Roundel*: "Vera Brittain was devastated by the death of both her fiancé, Roland Leighton, and her brother, Edward Brittain, in 1918. Her poem *Roundel* conveys both heartbreak and the dull ache of bitterness and loss. From the start, I knew that I wanted to set the poem for two voices so that we sense the presence of the lost person, and, as reinforced in the music, realise that part of the living partner has also died as they look towards their dead."

Just as Olaf was the voice in the cello.

My sister, Jojo, and I talk a great deal about our memories of Kit's life. But he also taught us about the mournful beauty of death. His unhappy end will always be muslin wrapped for me in the balm of Brahm's German Requiem and in the beauty of the cello that was the voice of Olaf Schmid.

Chapter 6
Words and Psalms

How long wilt thou forget me O Lord? For Ever?

—Psalm 13

I am reading an interview in *The Times* in January 2024 with the American actor Clarke Peters. He talks of his belief in the soul and demonstrates it with an unbearably painful memory of the death of his son, Guppy, from a tumour on his kidney. He was four years old. Peters described the light in the room changing as his son passed from life to 'what comes next'.

Peters' faith came from paternal grandmother and particularly from Psalm 100 "Make a joyful noise." It was the line chosen by Andrew Lloyd-Webber for his Coronation anthem. John Rutter too reaches naturally for the Psalms as the source for compositions, as did Brahms, for they are the poetry of human despair and divine consolation.

The former Conservative minister Jonathan Aitken discovered the Psalms when he was sent to prison for perjury, and under the influence of reading them, sought atonement and redemption, eventually become a prison chaplain. He has written a book about the Psalms for those feeling pressure in, among other places, the boardroom. Aitken once worked in the Treasury and still has his admirers within his Conservative party so perhaps a triumph to come would be a Psalm for Budget day.

He recommends Psalms for depression (42, 43 and 83), penitence (51), gratitude (16), and love of God's goodness (23). But the most one singular for darkness and despair is Psalm 130, the penitential De Profundis:

"Out of the depths have I called to you O Lord! Lord hear my voice."

De Profundis gave solace to Aitken, and a century earlier to Oscar Wilde; it was the title of his letter to his lover, Lord Alfred Douglas, written from Reading jail.

Psalms come naturally to choristers and particularly to Kit because he was more interested in words than some of his contemporaries.

One of them, Peter White, wrote to me about his abiding memory of their time together: "At the choir school, I chiefly remember his infectious sense of fun, and beneath the cassock and surplus, an almost fully fledged Kit was waiting to burst out. He loved music of course, to a certain extent we all did—our life revolved round a busy schedule of cathedral services—but for Kit, even then, words were equally fascinating. I had somehow acquired a small transistor radio and occasionally, we would catch *Just a Minute* with Kenneth Williams in full flight."

"Kit would be in hysterics and awe in equal measure and after lights out in senior dorm, we would hold impromptu rounds of our own *Just a Minute* with a torch checking the progress of the second hand. Inevitably, the promised whispers would crescendo to a clearly audible mezzo forte as Kit warmed to his subject, and, just as inevitably, hilarity would be quashed by the unreformed punishment system that was a feature of 1960s prep schools."

The actor and director Simon Callow also gave an address at the funeral teasing Kit over his attention to words, not just in the screenplay he wrote of EM Forster's novel *Maurice* but also for *Die Fledermaus* for the Scottish Opera in 1988.

Callow said: "Kit was unquestionably a lord of language, brilliant, bawdy, epigrammatic, erudite and he was not only wonderfully witty but he was also fanatical about the precision of his words…he was always complaining that the actors, the singers, didn't make enough of the words and I did point out that there was this small thing called the music as well, which he finally admitted was the case."

Kit's best case for words before music were the Psalms on which his choral childhood was based. He reached for them easily. When Julian was first missing on the mountain, Kit's reference was Elijah on the mountain. Our worst imaginings were Julian alone, battling a storm. Kit replied that Julian would not be alone and that his companion would be.

coverest with light as with a garment

Who stretchest out the heavens like a curtain.

After Kit's funeral, I looked up the reference.

Psalm 104

Bless the Lord, O my soul, O Lord my God thou art very great; thou art clothed with honour and majesty.

Who coverest thyself with light as with a garment: who stretchest out the heavens like a curtain. Who layeth the beams of his chambers in the waters: who maketh the clouds his chariot: who walketh upon the wings of the wind: Who makes his angels spirits; his ministers a flaming fire: Who laid the foundations of the earth, that it should not be removed for ever. Thou coverests it with the deep as with a garment: the waters stood above the mountains.

The Psalms mean 'the words accompanying the music', and there are about a hundred and fifty of them. Most movingly are those of exile either of territory or spirit. Critics date them within memory of 586 BCE when the Jewish people were exiled to Babylon.

I was reminded of this during the war on Israel and in Gaza which broke out in October 2023. A new war between two dispossessed people, begun by an act of terror against Israel. The crossing into Egypt took on a biblical significance of Israelite slavery in Egypt, freed by Moses in Exodus 3.7 and of Babylonian Captivity, in the book of Ezra.

Robert Alter writes in his commentary on the Book of Psalms that death is evoked in the imagery of drowning, although consolation is also found in the imagery of water.

I remember thinking of this apparent contradiction in Elizabeth Bishop's poem, *I am in Need of Music.* Somehow the lines about melody, 'deep, clear, and liquid slow', eclipsed the wretched image of my brother's brains floating in the bath.

Compare the lines from psalm 69: "Save me of God; for the waters are come in unto my soul. I sink in deep mire, where there is no standing: I am come into deep waters, where the floods overflow me…"

With this verse from Psalm 42: "As a deer yearns for the streams of water, so I yearn for You, O God."

Or, "The Lord is my shepherd…He leadeth me to the quiet waters by…"

Or Psalm 29: "The voice of the Lord is upon the waters: the Glory of God thundereth: the Lord is upon many waters."

Or Psalm 46: "Though the waters thereof roar and be troubled, though the mountains shake with the swelling thereof Selah. There is a river, the streams whereof shall make me glad the city of God, the holy place of the tabernacles of the most High."

Or Psalm 65: "Thou visitest the earth, and waterest it: thou greatly enrichest it with the river of God, which is full of water."

And Psalm 93: "The Lord on high is mightier than the noise of many waters, yea, than the mighty waves of the sea."

The composer, Errollyn Wallen, who writes so well of loss and of living among the departed, has a Psalm like longing for water: she says that she needs to be near water in order to compose and lives in a light house.

"The inspiration of water underlines most of my music and I need to be next to it, part of it, in it. I often think that if I could spend enough time looking out to sea and notate it in all its dancing torment record its formidable serenity only then would I have cracked the secrets of music. I think the same thing when I look up at the night sky up here in Scotland too. So much of the universe's water is produced as a by-product of star formation."

C. S. Lewis writes at the start of his book *Reflections on the Psalms* that he writes as an amateur. I write with precisely no knowledge or authority whatsoever but with only a glimpse of the beauty of the Psalms in the context of losing Kit. He may have been a modern libertine who wrote a stinging satire about Leviticus but his heart was in Evensong.

C. S. Lewis lays out the first premise of the Psalms. They were written by poets from the reign of David and some believe, with no historical evidence but perhaps evidence of deeper poetry, Psalm 18 to have been written by David.

"The Lord is my rock, my fortress and my deliverer,

My God is my rock, in whom I take refuge,

My shield and the horn of my salvation, my stronghold."

C. S. Lewis has a kindly mild position on the theme of Judgement on the psalms. He speaks for the Church of England in his preference for the word mercy—I too love the sequence of grace, mercy, and peace.

He makes the point that the oppressed seek justice and therefore, judgement, and it has a particular resonance for Jewish people. Yet Lewis turns away from the self-righteous and vindictive psalms as jarring to a modern ear.

"To be sure, the hates which we fight against in ourselves do not dream of quite such appalling revenges. We live at least in some countries we still live in a milder age. These poets lived in a world of savage punishments, of massacre and violence or blood sacrifice in all countries and human sacrifice in many."

I think of the attack by Hamas on a peaceful Jewish music festival and the suffering unleashed from thereon and I wonder at C. S. Lewis assertion that we live in a milder age. The lamentation element of the Psalms, and anguish of endurance feels the correct response: "And You, Oh Lord, How Long?" Commentators have noted that the war over this territory, feels unlike any other. Of course, it is the Holy Land.

At the Christmas Procession at Norwich Cathedral in 2023, the Dean wrote: "We have come together as Christmas draws very near to prepare ourselves for our celebration of the birth of God's beloved son. We gather together conscious of the darkness that besets our world and that the lands that Jesus walked are still deeply troubled."

The most Church of England Psalm is probably 23, which is also the public's favourite hymn.

"The Lord is my shepherd; I shall not want
He maketh me to lie down in green pastures:
He leadeth me beside the still waters.
He restoreth my soul: he leadeth me in the paths of righteousness for his name's sake.
Yea, though I walk through the valley of the shadow of death, I will fear no evil:
For thou art with me; thy rod and thy staff they comfort me.
Thou preparest a table before me in the presence of mine enemies:
Thou annointest my head with oil; my cup runneth over.
Surely goodness and mercy shall follow me all the days of my life:
And I will dwell in the house of the Lord forever."

"The image of the shepherd is pastoral and consoling. 'Quiet waters' is perhaps my favourite phrase in the Psalms."

C. S. Lewis notes that death has a finality in some of the Psalms which does not seem to convey the joy of an afterlife.

I find the Psalms, which are the poetic equivalent of the tolling bell satisfying because it is how grief feels. C. S. Lewis cites psalm 89 verses 46–49 as an example of human desolation.

How long, Lord? Will thou hide thyself forever?

Shall thy wrath burn like fire?

Remember how short my time is: wherefore hast thou made all men in vain?

What man is that he liveth and shall not see death? Shall he deliver his soul from the hand of the grave? Selah.

The author examines the motive of Judaism, is it for a better life on earth or, in the manner of ancient Egyptians, is it wrapped up in the afterlife?

He concludes with a compelling argument for the momentum of Judaism.

"Century after century, by blows which seem to us merciless, by defeat, deportation and massacre, it was hammered into the Jews that earthly prosperity is not in fact certain or even the probable reward of seeing God...But the astonishing thing is that the religion is not destroyed. In its best representatives, it grows purer, stronger and more profound. It is being, by this terrible discipline, directed more and more to its real centre."

C. S. Lewis goes on to discuss the psalms of praise and joy but I like to stick to desolation because it is where I think they have the most direct resonance.

The service I feel most affecting is Evensong at Ely Cathedral on Good Friday. There is no welcome and the choir files out also in silence. There is no organ. I sit in the choir stalls because this is not a service that attracts much of an audience. But attending once after the death of my father and the following year, after the death of Kit and Julian, I find the solemnity awe-inspiring.

One of the choristers, with a mop of dark hair, caught my eye and was clearly puzzled by the tears meandering down my cheeks. It was as if almost sixty years had been waved away and I was back in Canterbury Cathedral.

The theme that stays with me is the relationship between darkness and light. I have seen them as opposites, but, like sorrow and joy, Psalm 139 says both at once.

Verse 8

"If I say, Surely the darkness shall cover me; even the night shall be light about me. Yea, the darkness hideth not from three: but the night shineth as the day: the darkness and the light are both alike to thee."

The funeral prayer that we chose for Kit was by John Donne, on the same theme of darkness and light becoming one.

"Bring us, O Lord God, at our last awaking
Into the house and gate of heaven,
To enter into that gate and dwell in that house,
Where there shall be
No darkness nor dazzling, but one equal light;
No noise nor silence, but one equal music;
No fears nor hopes, but one equal possession;
No ends nor beginnings, but one equal eternity;
In the habitations of thy majesty and glory,
World without end."

Chapter 7
A Note from Kit's Lake Ely

Painting by Kit of the lake

Sometimes, Kit would arrive late for Sunday lunch saying that he had forgotten the time because he had been at a lake at Ely. Because of my adherence to timetables, I would respond grumpily and take his lunch out of the warming oven. Kit operated on creative time and I followed time management.

He suggested that we took a picnic to the lake so that he could show me and I calculated forty-five minutes each way. Because our parents had recently moved into a nursing home about forty-five minutes in the other direction I thought my visiting Ely lake would be an indulgence. One terrible aspect of the death of a loved one is the clarity of errors in hindsight.

Gus, Kit's daughter, had been there with him. Both were at a low ebb and their spirits were not improved when Kit's transit van became stuck at the bottom of the muddy track and they were not sure they would be leaving the lake. Kit made a melodramatic gamble with fate. He told Gus that if they could push the van up the hill and onto the road, their fortunes would turn. At that moment, a figure Gus called Tony the poet emerged to help and the van moved.

After Kit died, I began to think about the lake. I enquired about the basic facts of it. It turned out to be part of an area of one time clay pits worked for hundred and fifty years before being abandoned, exhausted, late in the 20th century. The pits filled with water from river Ouse, the wounds of industry healed, natural life returned. As trains rattle past and light industry continues nature triumphs.

The lake was offered for sale by the Environment Agency in 2020 and Kit introduced his close friend, Caroline Roboh, who bought it in order to return it to its natural state and to secure its future.

Their shared motto was the from John Betjeman poem, *Trebethrick*: "Ask for our children all the happy days you gave."

Caroline recovered a trail of emails from Kit. First the campaigning emails against Network Rail over plans to build. Kits quixotic battles for social justice were to me his worst abuses of time management. He wasted precious hours fighting Transport for London over regular congestion zone and parking fines. At Kit's funeral, the Mayor of London, Sadiq Khan, sent a funny and warmly human message, which got a round of applause.

He wrote: "Kit's loss will be mourned by his family, friends and fans. But nowhere will his absence be more acutely felt than in the office of the Transport for London's Chief Finance Officer."

Kit had managed to get a preservation tree order on a ropey looking oak and I thought it a characteristic touch of his that he traced it to a Nordic king.

His keep out sign at the gate to the lake made me laugh out loud. He would have agonised over the right shade of aqua blue green and had written in a poetic font:

"This woodland, lake and reedbed habitat is under conservation as a breeding ground for bittern, otter, nightingale, tern, and other endangered wetland species. Admission to the reserve is by written arrangement only at warden@rosewellreserve.co.uk. Please keep to the legally designated statuary public footpath. Thank you."

Nearby was an old style sign by the environment agency. 'No Public Access' written on a warning red background. You get the picture. But Caroline invited me to help her maintain the lake as a kind of memorial to Kit and a legacy for his children and suddenly, I had all the time in the world.

A bird survey, recorded geology from the late Jurassic age and more interesting for Kit, "a mosaic of habitats within the site supports a variety of breeding birds associated with open waters, including nationally important numbers of bittern."

It also recorded at least thirteen species, including mute swan, gadwall, little grebe, and great crested grebe. The scattered scrub provided nesting habitat for bittern, marsh harrier, bearded tit, reed warbler, sedge warbler, reed bunting and cuckoo.

Jo Thomas from the Wildfowl and Wetlands Trust (The Fens) enchanted Kit and he would fondly imitate her rising inflexion on the subject of bittern.

I had an idea of following Kit's pilgrim route as a tribute to him but squinting at the illustrated map produced days after he died for Kit's family and friends by my son Henry in an act of wonderful thoughtfulness, I could see the issue of reconciling pilgrimages with BUSY people.

Most felt a day would do it. So I came up with a pilgrim menu: Day one, a visit to Kit's lake, prayers at Kit's church in Stoke Ferry, Spotify music of Mendelssohn and Charles Villiers Stanford, and back to my house for fizz, cakes and a blasting of Kit's hits from his old CD cassette.

Day two, an actual pilgrimage along a pilgrim route to King's Lynn, and a pilgrim feast at the Hanseatic home of Kit's dear friends, Simon Thurley and Anna Keay.

Thus, day one pilgrims arrived on a beautiful May Friday at the locked gate to the lake, where Kit's aqua-green notice was positioned. The environment agency building was closed. We had no key.

So we pole vaulted over it towards the downward grassy path, the areas of scrub, and a view that made tears spring to my eyes. Of course, now I understood what this meant to Kit. The beautifully misshapen lantern form of Ely Cathedral right there in front of us. It felt like the pilgrim route Kit would have imagined for it was a Danish invader, the devout Christian King Cnut, who in 1016, saw Ely rise first as an abbey church and then a cathedral. Its shape is unmistakeable.

In his book, *Ships of Heaven*, Christopher Somerville writes:

"It's sunset silhouette is all spikes, turrets, square tower tops, and pinnacles at disjointed intervals. It looks massively lopsided."

"There's a basic shape to all cathedrals and it is based on symmetry; a recumbent cross shape, with a central nave as the main stem and transepts of equal length composing the arms."

"Ely Cathedral does not conform. Either part of it is missing or there's too much of it on the left hand side. It looks eccentric, multiform and haunting, a ship of the line shattered by broadsides, limping back to harbour after some tremendous battle."

The ship of the fens, in a land that was once marsh and waterways, and here a secret lake.

We sought the waters' edge but Gus remembered that Kit's spot was further down and finally we found it through scrub and bramble.

A derelict rowing boat, which Kit had dragged up the Ouse, gave it away. And there was the little ladder in the reeds he would use to slip into the water.

We laid out a blanket, I found some warm prosecco and ham and cheese and the potter, and life force Emma Bridgewater produced, stunningly, steel thimbles of martini cocktails, a proper tribute to Kit.

In the middle of the lake was a platform dominated by gulls and already Caroline and I were fretting about ecological balance. How could we make room for the terns?

There were other signs of neglect. Some of the grassy paths were now impassable. On the other side of the lake, heavy trees would change the nature of the water, eventually to swamp. There were shouts and whoops as groups brought dogs, equipment, litter to the shore. This was part nature reserve, part street party.

Somehow, what we wanted was a spiritual retreat, something that wove together the final threads of Kit's life. Pilgrimages, nature, music. A journey up a river, a lake, a cathedral.

Caroline phoned me a few weeks later saying she wondered how we could change the name from Roswell Pits to Kit's Lake. It was already Kit's lake so far as we were concerned but now we have to realise the wistful description of it on his notice.

After Caroline and I held our first teams meeting with the kindly, modest, deeply knowledgeable Jo, she wrote back to us.

My own personal views about Roswell Pit are as follows:

It is a lovely tranquil place and worth keeping a corner of the site nice and tranquil, especially when there are public footpath routes elsewhere. Bitterns and marsh harriers both appreciate peace and quiet. The reed fringes around Roswell Pit are probably not broad enough (from memory) to support a breeding pair of either yet, but reeds are inclined to spread so one or the other species could breed in the future. Either could use the site from time to time.

Scrub: I would consider managing this on a rotation. Just check what the best rotation would be for nightingales, likely to be on a eight to ten year rotation would be fine. It will grow back incredibly quickly and form dense low-lying new growth areas for nightingales to feed in and other species including warblers like Whitethroat and Blackcap (and many more).

I'd avoid having a bonfire on any good bits of grassland. Reusing an existing fire site may work or deciding to establish one on an area that's been covered in dense scrub for years where it would be hard to bring back the species rich grassland.

If you want to keep scrub habitat managed on a rotation, one other thing to consider is to leave some of the cut stems and branches to afford a bit of protection from nibbling muntjac. Some people use the scrub to form what is referred to as a dead-hedge too.

Grassland: I'd try to retain the grassland areas you currently have. It has a nice diverse array of plant species. Ideally, if the areas could be cut, the cuttings removed to keep the soil fertility lower. Cuttings placed under some dense scrub where diverse grassland plant species won't grow.

Bird Boxes: I wouldn't go mad but having a few high up open-fronted boxes for Spotted Flycatcher in the mature trees would be a good idea.

Tern raft: If gulls are becoming a problem, try to take the rafts out of the water and place them back in the water a little later, just as the common terns arrive back on their breeding grounds. This may give the terns more of a chance to acquire space first.

Having some organised guided walks would be a great idea, rather than opening up access fully.

Providing some interpretation: This may be nice to do. Before printing any signage if you want to knock something into the ground I would check this out with Natural England first as part of the site is notified for geology. Or you may prefer to print a leaflet and provide a box on the side of an existing post?

Writing a brief site management plan for Roswell Pit: I think would be a great idea and I would see if perhaps Ely Wildspace may be able to help you draft one. If you write this document, it could include a few hand drawn annotated map and a timeframe for works. I'd send it to Natural England as they may have some helpful comments/advice and it would be good for them to see prior to asking them to consent it. This document could cover a three to five year period?

Your reedbed area: I visited the site in the breeding season, so I didn't access the reedbed to avoid disturbance to Marsh Harrier and Bittern that could potentially have been breeding in there at the time. From memory, though, and talking to someone else who knew the site I believe the reedbed could do with some management to improve it.

Over time, if reedbeds are not managed the stems/reed litter builds up and this can lead to eventual drying out of a reedbed and for scrub and willow to start to grow. It will try and transition into a wet woodland and if it were to do that, you'd lose the breeding Bittern and Marsh Harrier.

Reedbed leaf litter can be good for some species, including invertebrates.

I would try and get a bit of expert advice on this. Start off with Natural England and see where that leads. Speak to them about funding also, if they can think of any suitable sources.

Subject to assessing the site, working out what is there and the best plan of action, it may be a project that could require heavy duty machinery like diggers to restore or create some channels. I'm not sure how to gain access to that reedbed area either, so it would need some thought putting into this and potentially it could cost quite a bit of money, subject to how dry the reedbed gets by late summer.

Once again, I'm sorry this email didn't send, but I do hope this information helps to get you off to a flying start!

Kit would be extremely proud of you both and your efforts, I'm very sure of that.

Jo

Waterscape Manager (The Fens)

Wildfowl & Wetlands Trust (WWT)

It is the unexpected and kindly references to Kit that always make my eyes blur. But here was his legacy. I am a journalist by background and the idea of a five year plan sounded beyond comprehension. But I am learning a different sense of time, Kit's time scale, and I could imagine him willing me on.

As I looked across the water to the other side, beneath the cathedral, I thought of the bidding prayer from the Festival on Nine Lessons and Carols: "Lastly, let us remember before God all those who rejoice with us, but upon another shore and in a greater light, that multitude which no person can number, whose hope was in the Word make flesh and who we for evermore as one."

I find a watercolour that Kit has painted of the lake, with a swan in the foreground and the cathedral dominating the horizon. And I remember his lyrics to *Swansong*, set to the later part of *The Swan* from Le Carnaval des Animaux by Camille Saint-Saens:

Fairy liquid squeegees and dismembered brollies, Coca Cola cans and rusting shopping trollies,

Several discarded single black 'Doc Martens' hordes and hordes of old McDonald's cartons,

Half a Fiat 126 to claim the insurance, prophylactics way beyond mankind's endurance,

Tesco bags and bits of orange nylon rope.

And look...

There...

Are...

Bottles labelled Cherryade and Rocket Thunder, empty packs of cigarettes and Golden Wonder,

Toys that you get given free at service stations, plastic fobs form Henley members' reservations,

Orange peel and Castrol superlube containers, Bacofoil and Adidas athletic trainers, double blad disposable blue razor blades...

And look...

There...

Are...

Part disintegrating bits of perch and tench

and floating recent life that won't bear close attention,

shiny pools of manganese and benzo-chloride

sulphurous waves of petro-fluoride,

sewage treated

and untreated

In profusion, draining from an engine sump in part solution,

Old car batteries sitting on the glorious placid shoreline

Leaking acid

And washed down from lovely, shimmering Derwentwater

One whole sheep marked 'radioactive do not slaughter'

Canisters with skull and crossbones part revealed

Canisters unmarked just saying Sellafield

Banks of vegetation standing, rotting sweetly, banks where vegetation's given up completely

There...I sat...down...and

I saw a swan of purest whiteness gently lying, saw a swan of purest whiteness slowly dying

Saw a swan enmeshed in bits of angler's twine…poisoned by the lead weights on a fishing line,

And many people rushing forward who cried to see it

Many people rushing forward to try to free it,

Saw the swan, who lifted up her failing head saw them gasp together as she quietly said

"You'll no doubt have heard how swans refrain from crying, up until the moment that we find

We're dying, charming but as you can see by then it's not much use, quite apart from which swans aren't responsible you know…

So…

What's…

Your…

Excuse?"

It was Socrates who wrote of swans who perceiving their death, sing more and better than ever they did before. It was a metaphor for immortality of the soul, which of course, Kit would have known, theologically and musically. And I discover that Avo Part composed a Swansong in 2013, the final notes faltering as the swan dies. It is based on Cardinal Newman's sermon Wisdom and Innocence, from which the funeral prayer we said for Kit is derived.

"Oh Lord, support us all the daylong of this troublous life, Until the shadows lengthen and the evening comes and the busy world is hushed and the fever of life is over and our work is done. Then Lord in thy mercy Grant us a safe lodging a holy rest And peace at the last."

Caroline and I decide to make *Swansong* the anthem for Kit's lake. And I think again of Sibelius's swan of Tuonela and Wagner and Edvard Grieg and Stringberg and once we get mute swans back on the lake, I shall read out Henrik Ibsen's poem, *A Swan*, written in 1859.

My pure white swan,

Silent and quiet;

Neither wingflaps nor bird's trills

Let your voice be known.

The dying swan is woven through history, myth, and music, and here it is again at Kit's lake, again representing serenity and otherworldliness. I make Christmas cards printed with Kit's painting, and with the words of *Swansong* on the back of them.

Anna is also practising with her choir Cambridge Voices for our plan for a concert at Ely Cathedral following our pilgrimage. She is rehearsing on a Saturday in November when she messages me with a link to Charles Villiers Stanford Bluebird.

"I just practised this beautiful song for tomorrow which has been sprung upon us last minute and it made me think of Kit."

The lake lay blue below the hill
O'er it, as I looked, there flew
Across the waters, cold and still
A bird whose wings were palest blue
The sky above was blue at last
The sky beneath me blue in blue
A moment, 'ere the bird had
Passed
It caught his image as he flew.

I reminded her that Charles Stanford was Kit's favourite composer and that it must be a sign, if there were such a thing.

On a cold November day, with the sky daubed in a moody dark palette but the beech trees falling leaves warm ochres and tangerines, Kim and I drive to Cambridge to the Victorian All Saint's Church, its walls and windows of pre-Raphaelite design, to watch Cambridge Voices.

Anna had already warned me about Blue Bird, but my tears trickled onto the programme sheet the moment the soprano voice soared from the back of the church—what Kit would once have sung as a treble—as if the slow wings of a bird above the lake. The other song in flight was the *Falcon Carol* (Corpus Christi) by Benjamin Britten, words anonymous.

"Ah, He bare him up, he bare him down, he bare him into an orchard brown. Lully, lullay, lullay, lullay. The falcon hath borne my mate away. In that orchard, there was an hall that was hanged with purple and pall. And in that hall there was a bed: it was hanged with gold so red. In an that bed, there lieth a knight, his wounds bleeding by day and night. By that bedside there kneeleth a maiden, and she weepeth both night and day. And by that bedside there standeth a stone 'Corpus Christi' written thereon. Ah!"

Both the Blue Bird and the Falcon end on a disappearing note. I think of the unfinished requiems by Beethoven and Mozart and the pen dropping from the hand of Bach.

Somehow music, like the birds leaving us behind, is a soul in flight.

The following week, we are back at the lake, gloriously glassy on a still cold day. The clouds form mirror snowcapped peaks in the water. Caroline brings with her a friend, the French photographer Ferrante Ferranti, who tactfully compares his stunning iPhone compositions of afternoon light on Ely Cathedral and lake with my photographs of Caroline's foot and water without reflection.

Yet even I cannot mess up the contours of the cathedral in front of the sunset at the far end of the dove grey water. We are meeting here Ed Pope, a gentle patrician figure with merry eyes who is advising us on bird life.

Ed's father set up a nature reserve called Kingfisher Bridge, a wetlands, and he has gone further with a safari reserve near Kings Lynn. The native landscape is happy to accommodate water buffalo.

For us, he recommends keeping the trees low to allow nesting and encourage song birds with fine millet seed. He suggests we use diggers to create banks in order to bring in waders. And the platforms lovingly erected in the middle of the lake to house terns (which should in tern chase away mink) are instead being dominated by gulls. The best thing would be to remove them for a year.

He also muses on draining the lake a bit, releasing water back into the river. We wonder where the two meet and I remember Kit talking of dragging his rowing boat through a tunnel. Sure enough, on the other side is a water underpass which reaches the river.

We also discuss the delicate issue of public access without dogs and noise to disturb the turtle doves we are planning. How could we put this politely on a public notice?

"Beware adders?" Ed suggests mischievously.

Hit list: Grebes, great crested grebes, waders, common redshanks, ringed and little ringed plovers, little kingfisher! Create sand martin nests?

Bramble and scrub hawthorn hedges around wetland area six species of warblers common whitethroat, blackcap, garden warbler willow warbler, common chiff chaff, sky larks, little owls, tawny owls, barn owls, winter lapwings, mute swan.

Season

April: Pied Avocet, black tailed Godwit

May: Godwit, spotted redshank, common sandpiper, common greenshank

July: Green sandpiper

August: Dunlin, Ruff, common greenshank, green sandpiper, wood sandpiper

September: Little stint, curlew sandpiper, dunlin, ruff, spotted redshank and common greenshank.

I examine The Kingfishers' Bridge Wetland Creation Trust charity.

Birds

Sixty-five bird species bred in 2008

Bittern (four blooming males, three nests, one or two young recorded)

Marsh Harriet (three nests, five young reared)

Water rail (six plus pairs)

Little Ringed Plover (one pair one young reared from two broods)

Lapwing (at least seven pairs attempted, five young reared)

Snipe (six displaying birds—an increase)

Redshank (about six pairs)

Black headed gulls (thousand yikes)

Common terns

Turtle dove

Barn owls

Tawny owl (six territories)

Sand Martin

A good year for warblers

Cetti's warbler (two singing females assumed breeding first time)

Sedge Warblers (thirty-seven singing males)

Reed Warblers (eighty-three singing males—an increase)

Bearded tits (five pairs but few juveniles around)

BT nest box erected March 2007 inspected Sep 2008 found to contain two bearded tit nests including two unhatched eggs. Nest material included hundred and thirty-five feathers (including those of greylag goose, coot, mallard, teal, bittern, water rail, plus water buffalo hair).

So far rather disappointing late summer/autumn wader passage except green sandpipers and snipe, up to thirty much in evidence enjoying water buffalo wallows.

Up to fourteen little egrets

A great white heron 28 Sep

Up to two hundred and fifty-five greylag geese and two hundred and sixty-six Canada geen, one snow goose. Up to thirty siskins.

Plants

Fend pondweed and purple small reed, water pennywort—invasive North American aquatic. Water germander, fen ragwort, Cambridge milk parsley.

Insects

Potentially, a new moth along with a restricted range beetle. The musk beetle, large iridescent green longhorn beetle, two hundred and thirty-seven species of macro moths.

Future projects

We are hoping to improve the seventy-five acres of wash land for breeding waders

Guiding principles

To maximise a diversity of approach to habitat creation and management.

To learn and build new techniques for good science.

To share good practice.

David Bellamy wrote

"The fens are one of my most favourite parts of Britain, a watery wonderland bursting with a very special sort of biodiversity that has been in the care of marshman and their families for millennia. All set about with horizons that take your breath away. Kingfishers' Bridge is a shining example of what I like to call the green renaissance, an organic landscape put back in good heart by a farming family who are about their heritage."

The great supporter was Robin Page, a crater faced countryman whom I came across thirty years ago when I was editing the *Sunday Telegraph* and he was a columnist. He took against me then as a flighty metropolitan woman, which I guess I was. How things come round.

As the blackthorn and then the hawthorn hedges start to blossom, a year after Kit's death, his daughter Gus takes her baby son Ernie for his first walk to the river at Stoke Ferry. It is chilly and drizzling, but there is the sniff of spring in the air. Something makes her look back as she returns along the river path to the house. A swan is gliding down the river towards her.

And we do it. Cambridge Voices perform a programme entitled Byrd and Bird—sacred music and nature—in the Lady Chapel at Ely cathedral. The acoustics are unearthly.

Anna sings her first solo, the Silver Swan, by Orlando Gibbons, with ethereal purity.

"The silver swan who living had no note, when death approached, unlocked her silent throat;

Leaning her breast against the reedy shore, thus sung her first and last, and sung no more;

Farewell, all joys; Oh death, come close mine eyes; More geese than swans now live, more fools than wise."

Kits friend, the priest , introduces the performance

When Sarah asked me to say a few words by way of introduction tonight, I remembered a poem by James Fenton, the Oxford poet, journalist and critic, which begins:

What would the dead want from us?

Which of course led me to ponder what Kit might want of us,
What Kit might make of this evening,
Ever the showman,
he would obviously appreciate the idea of performance,
And ever the chorister,
He would applaud the programme,
And the skill and artistic excellence of the musicians ,
He would relish the chance to experience again
This magnificent Cathedral, which he knew so intimately.
But later in Fenton's poem come the lines.

I think the dead would want us
To weep for what they have lost.

I think that weeping can be something like the distillation
Of enjoying and remembering
Considering and celebrating all the connections with Kit
Which intersect here among us and in this performance,
The music, of course, sublime,
But somehow subtly tinged,
By the difficulties
Of Byrd's Catholic recusancy in a suspicious, Protestant age.
For Kit, a connection, as a composer with an individual who, against the
odds, lived what he believed, and managed to thrive and flourish.

Then, the family connection between Kit and Anna,
And through her, a keen interest in Cambridge Voices.
There is the avian connection in the title of this evening's performance
The name and the name
Sacred Music and Sacred Nature.

The lake we hope to restore will be not only a unique memorial
But also a regenerated site
To encourage and support a greater and more diverse community of birds
and other wildlife.

The water itself literally connects to the rivers which run through East
Anglia which Kit knew so well.

The rivers connect to the whole idea of pilgrimage
Something else close to his heart
And one of the many projects on which he was working at the time of his
death.
There is a flagstone dedicated to the pilgrims who came to Ely over the
centuries outside the Lady Chapel.

So yes we weep at the beauty and the logic and the poetry of it all.

Fenton's poem goes on:

And time would find them generous as they used to be

And what else would they want from us?

But an honoured place in our memory

A favoured room a hallowed chair

Privilege and celebrity

Celebrity? Definitely

And certainly the sense of Kit is still lingering

In those chairs and rooms where we knew him

Of his spirit informing what we are doing here tonight.

Privilege? Perhaps

But perhaps the privilege was ours.

The poem concludes with something between an invitation and challenge and wish.

A wish I share with you all and with Kit:

And there might be a pact between

Dead friends and living friends

What our dead friends would want from us

Would be such living friends.

Then I thought how proud Kit would have been of Anna, and if only, if only, if only he had known about his grandchildren born after he had died.

The time will come soon when he will no longer be my older brother, because I will have passed him in age, as my sister is already soon to do. We carry on and they do not, but I am trying to be a living friend.

Chapter 8
Constellations and Consolations

Bach is an astronomer, discovering the most marvellous stars. Beethoven challenged the universe. I only try to express the soul and the heart of man.

—Frederic Chopin

The story of the Cross of the Cosmos is a curious one. More than a couple of years ago, I was approached by the former Archbishop of Canterbury, Rowan Williams, about a processional Cross, designed by the artist David Montalto, which Dr Williams believed possessed divine properties.

While studying as a young artist in Florence in 1959, David experienced the first of eight visions, and over a lifetime, he worked on a Cross that expressed them. He designed a lamb encrusted with pearls against a blue enamel background with a halo and Cross of diamonds symbolising Christ.

At the top of the Cross is an oval relief depicting the Holy Trinity and below the roundel, God, arms outstretched to all. Emmanuel. On his lap, is the Holy Ghost represented as a dove.

The Cross abounds with symbols and when Rowan Williams first saw it in 2016, he proclaimed the theological symbolism 'beyond the knowledge' of the artist.

Finally, David managed to persuade NASA to donate some moon dust which is contained within the Cross of the Cosmos. It was consecrated in Westminster Abbey and the anthem, with words by Kit and music by Roderick Williams, was performed at Magdalene College, shortly after Kit died.

When I arrived at the chapel, my mind was a garish kaleidoscope of snap shots.

The torches uplighting the faces of the young policemen, sitting with my sister, Jojo, to tell our mother that Kit was dead, braced for her shudder of disbelief, meeting her eyes begging for it not to be true, the polite language of administration of the coroner's office, asking the grandchildren to be pall bearers, emptying Kit's canvas shoulder bag and giving his moleskin notebook of lyrics to James McConnel, breathing in the scent of Kit from one of his silk performance scarves.

The opening the door to Henry who had flown back from LA and then driven down to Norfolk to be with me, finding an unopened Christmas present from Kit to my comic writer daughter, Tilly, in brown paper and string, a biography of Dorothy Parker and the message, 'no pressure'. The gift of an annotated copy of *The Little Prince* for Gus, which she had regretfully thrown aside, because we all act in the present and not as if those we love will suddenly be gone.

But now Kit's death seemed to have prescience. What was the very last thing he wrote, what was he thinking about until the final moment? It was the cosmic order of the universe and the guiding intelligence behind it.

Vision of the Cross—for Baritone solo and full choir

Baritone
And I became aware of an angel
A youth with pale red hair
Who had come to ask of me a task
To create a cross, the Cross of the Cosmos

Choir
How can man's finite mind extend beyond infinity?
Baritone:
I considered the heav'ns earth's moon I saw and heard

Choir
The more our science might comprehend, the less we see

Baritone
In the beginning was the word...

Choir

What great consciousness or hand ordained that first explosion?
And decrees that which outlasts our sun beyond our end?

Baritone

Then I must do thy will

Choir

Thy will be done
Baritone
En ark heien ho logros
Choir:
An infinitely vaster mind has ordered time and space

Baritone

Kai ho logos en pros ton theon

Choir

What hubris, then, has ordered time and space?
What has realigned our given place?

Baritone

Kai theos en hologos

Choir

When science leads us to Wuhan, Chernobyl...
Shall not man declare—as he lays down his gun

Baritone

All beings tremble before violence
All fear death
All love life
All:
Thy will be done

Baritone

Is this eluctable?
I'm but one man
An atom, cosmic dust

Choir

A petriglass yet leaves us blind
We won't see face-to-face
Till faith can spring our finite mind
From reason's place

Baritone

Atoms are indestructible
Dust contains memory,
We need but trust

Choir

Where science cannot grant us sight
Illumined by a greater light

Baritone

Dust may be reordered
Dust we may restore

Choir

We yield our knowledge
Which is none
Thy will be done

Baritone

Transubstantiated from above by a higher consciousness

Choir

Yet in pursuit of finite power
On wings of wax man flies

Towards some new Hiroshima
And thus he dies

Baritone
Man's bigotries divide that which is the same
Whose name is love

Choir
Enraged by what he can't explain
Man bearing still the mark of cain

Baritone
Blasphemes while slaughtering his son

Choir
Thy will be done

Baritone
I will transform these atoms, then
Until I once again fulfil the pattern of design
I saw it gradually disappear and shine

Choir
Then greet this symbol of rebirth
Man's murderous device
Inheriting once more his earth through sacrifice

Baritone
The Cross of the Cosmos

Choir
That, newly humbled as the lamb
Man cries

All

"You were before I am"
And with the cosmos sings as one
Choir:
Thy will be done
Baritone:
Emmanuel!

Choir

God is with us
Thy will be done

The Vision of the Cross anthem spoke to order and radiance, as depicted by Bach or, earlier, in the psalms.

It recalls my favourite Psalm 104, verse 2:

Verse 2: *"The Lord wraps himself in light as with a garment,*
He stretches out the heavens like a tent
And lays the beams of his upper chamber on their waters.
He makes the clouds his chariot
And rides on the wings of the wind
He makes winds his messengers
Flames of fire his servants."

I think too of a passage by Jon Fosse, the Nordic writer who won the Nobel prize for literature this year.

A New Name (Septology)

"…it's really a cold clear night and I see the stars shining clearly up in space, and I see the moon, it's big and round and yellow, I think and I think that it's God shining from the moon, and from the stars, yes, in a way, even if he isn't anything, and doesn't have any how and doesn't have any why, yes, because God doesn't have a why any more than, yes, than the moon does, or the stars, the moon is just there, the stars are just there, yes, a flower is just there, and a deer, because both the moon and the stars and flowers just are what they are, but they have their how in opposition to God..."

And I think of constellations and consolations. I have found both on my Hanseatic pilgrimage in the year that Julian and Kit died.

The great event in the Hanseatic calendar is the annual June festival in the cathedral (always a cathedral) city of Torun in Poland, home of Copernicus.

Here, the medieval view of the universe was challenged by science.

I had arranged in Torun to meet Hamish Stewart, he of the vision of an east coast route of cycling Hansa Europeans, who had come with his wife to set up their stall.

My husband and I arrived late morning, shunted up the motorway by the tailgating Polish lorries. Our modern featureless hotel was called the Copernicus and in the lobby, we spotted a clever looking, grey-haired English couple poring over a town map. Outside, coaches were drawing up, one I saw from Lubeck. It was like the Eurovision Song Contest but for national costumes and sea shanties.

In the centre of Torun, were the familiar tall merchant houses, show windows displaying gingerbread, apothecaries, and down a pretty narrow lane one special townhouse, multi-storeyed, red brick with fine decoration crosses, clover, red black and white. It followed the pattern of upper floors for storage space.

Here was the home and intellectual universe of Copernicus. He was born here in 1473 when the medieval universe was restricted, with the greater expanse reserved for God. It was a strict separation between the territorial and the celestial.

Hell is the earth's fiery centre, purgatory a cone shaped mountain, Heaven is made of spheres ending in tenth Heaven, the Empyrean, God's domicile, the most blessed place of all.

Until the 14th century, scientific astronomy was the preserve of Islamic countries and it was the work of Islamic scientists, and Arab translations of Greek authors, that Copernicus built upon.

At the top of the house is the white room of Copernicus's compasses of Johannes Hevelius, the Polish Lithuania astronomer.

Copernicus's epiphany came from an exchange of ideas, which naturally happens through trading routes. Torun merchants transported salted herring and dried cod from Gdansk and brought in Southern European wine, olive oil, spices and cloth.

Silver, copper, and lead came from Cracow, wood from Southern Poland. It was Polish yew which was used by the English for manufacturing bows, as well as building Europe's churches.

Nicolaus Copernicus left Torun in 1491 to begin studies at Cracow, the trading, cultural, and scientific centre.

At the Academy of Cracow, he studied Aristotle, Heraclitus, Epicurus, Plato, Plutarch, Cicero, and the Pythagoreans. It was the studies of ancient philosophy which inspired Copernicus to become interested in the Earth's movement.

We think of Bach and his mathematical music of the spheres, but the Han dynasty (202 BC–9 AD), like the ancient Greeks, believed in the virtuous relationship between musical notes and the distance between the stars and the planets.

His work *On the Revolutions of the Heavenly Spheres* was published in 1543. It was written from the perspective of astronomy but also cosmology, a vision of the world and man's place in it. He considered theology and philosophy.

His work centred on patterns in movement of planets against the 'fixed stars' using geometry and mathematics for accuracy. This is what provoked the statement from the Catholic church on 5 March 1616.

"The false science of the Pythagoreans, completely contrary to the Holy Bible about moment of the Earth and the immobility of the Sun, propagated by Nicolaus Copernicus in the Revolutions of the Heavenly Spheres…in order to prevent such science from spreading to the detriment of the Catholic truth, it has been considered appropriate to suspend the aforementioned work."

His book was thus published by Protestants in Amsterdam, another dimension to the Reformation.

The figure of Copernicus dominates Torun, literally, for a giant puppet is the star of the Hanseatic festival.

While I have been sitting reflecting on the movement of the stars in Copernicus's study, the Hansa markets have been setting up in sight of the Teutonic castle ruins looking out at the river.

This is a living museum, with wooden figures of monks, and carvings of battlements and angels, ship rope and wooden crosses.

A woman wanders past, dressed in a lime green medieval dress with long sleeves and a high cone hat. Perfectly normal. In a playground, boys in football strips chat on high wooden thrones with crusader crosses on them. Below on a created football pitch, boys whack the ball against a medieval wall.

Nearby, is the magnificent red brick 14th century Gothic St James Gothic church, which became a parish church for the city of Torun and a sanctuary on the pilgrimage to St James's grave in the cathedral of Santiago De Compostela in Spain.

The city of Copernicus also managed to accommodate Reformation. Mid-14th century, the Teutonic Knights handed the church to Cistercian nuns. As Martin Luther's ideas swept along the Hanseatic route, the Protestants took over the church.

As I stand at the back, looking up at the delicately drawn ceiling above the high Gothic churches, a priest is conducting Catholic Communion.

In the old town square, the delegations are gathering for the 43rd International Hanseatic Day. On an assembled stage in a market square, enthusiasts have changed into pale blue shirts and sailor caps, and are launching into sea shanties.

The men and women of the Stader Hafensanger, sturdy and jolly, are swaying along to accordions and holding circular life belts.

In the corner of their eyes, they can see a gigantic and slightly unstable Copernicus on wheels being dragged along the street. The crowd's attention shifts to this figure, the size of a two storey building and holding an iron globe in the path of the sun. Some stop and smile, others continue their business. The Poles are phlegmatic about their history except for reverence for Copernicus and Chopin.

A little self-consciously some new figures in fancy dress have joined the onlookers.

Women are wearing aprons and caps, a priest strikes up a staged conversation with a beggar, several knight strike poses wrapped capes of chivalric orders.

The distant sound of pipers comes from a nearby street and suddenly, we are watching a parade. Here they come with their banners saying Visby, Krakow, Straupe, Cesis.

Women in long velvet dresses, tassel belts, and head bands, men in tunics, and to my husband's delight, women majorettes with tassels.

The definition of Hanseatic costume has become elastic.

Polish police fold muscular arms and watch from the shop doorways, more knights more banners of dragons and castles, Gdansk, Hanover, Braunschweig, Torun, waving Koszalen, Straupe, Lubeck Chelmno.

But where is King's Lynn?

Stade, Alfeld, Stralsund, Stendal, Ruthen, Kalmar, Demmin, Hamburg, Osnaburck, Wismar, Limbazi, Neuss, Wesel, Hamm, Kyritz, Hasselt, Frankfurt, slightly embarrassed smiles, Luneburg, Brugge, Bergen.

Men with trumpets, a brass band and finally, I spot Hamish and his wife, the only representatives of the sea power of Great Britain.

Meanwhile, the orchestra is gathering in the Hanseatic castle grounds. With appropriate dignity, the Mayor of Torun and of Lubeck, who is President of the Hansa, take to the stage. The welcome the footsore parade who are now laying down their banners and taking up their seats within the castle wall. As evening falls, there a performance of Holst's Jupiter, as a nod to science.

We peel off for a plate of salami and cheese, wandering back along the cobbled streets to the hotel, past more soaring churches and cathedrals, a café shop window in which a sinister doll sits at a table with a canvas and easel, and shops selling gingerbread.

Email from Hamish

Apologies for not getting back to you earlier. We have had a nightmare with our leaflets and banners on the stand. The customs here in Poland kept them and would not release them. They eventually did but charged us two hundred and twenty pounds for the duty. As the products were to be returned to the UK they were not subject to duty but sadly we had to pay it.

The customs also stole hundred rather nice Hansa pens but they denied it so there is nothing we can do about it.

We eventually got to the stand products at 9.30 this morning and the show opened at 10, so a mad rush to get everything up. It then rained heavily to add to the fun, so it wasn't a great start. But life improved and we had a lot of interest in our cultural route.

Hamish Stewart

Hansa Beverley

If Hamish gets his way and the Hansa route blazes across the east coast of the UK, it will end in Shetland, so far north that it is practically Norway. During the medieval age, it belonged to Norway and even today, its flag looks Norwegian and its culture is Norse/Celtic, celebrating fiddlers and fires. The flat, marshy windswept landscape is interspersed with fishing villages of solid stone and Scandinavian brightly coloured cabins.

Shetland's oldest pub, the Booth, markets itself still as a sanctuary for artists I was keen to end my Hanseatic search there, not least because my friend, Frank Strang, has, through sheer will, established a space port, Saxavord, in the most northerly stretch.

The journey is about the same as to St Petersburg, by the times we have flown to Glasgow then to Sumburgh airport, and two ferries more to reach Unst. It is so remote here that the rockets will fire vertically and only seals or puffins in the north Atlantic will take any notice. We stay at an old RAF base watching winds whip up the waves along the pebbled coastline and gazing at stars in a clear dark sky. In the morning, we get into truck driven by the station manager and look at the steel girders and platform which form the basis of the space port.

I first met Frank through the science festival which I co-organise in Braemar; astrophysicists pack into the village hall to discuss with much geniality, the end of the human race. One year Lord Rees, the Astronomer Royal, was on stage with Dame Jocelyn Bell Burnell, who had observed the first radio pulsars in space, emitted from neutron stars. Dame Jocelyn had a fiercely realistic approach to her work, based on years of working round the constraints of family life and perhaps being Scottish. Yet she also studied the poetry of the stars.

Many cosmologists have a sense of wonder which is sympathetic to religion although not of it. Lord Rees, the Astronomer Royal, for instance, describes himself as "a practising but unbelieving Christian."

Asked whether he believes in God, he answers, "I do not, but I share a sense of wonder and mystery with many who do."

In the stampede for space among billionaires and governments, it is left to cosmologists such as Lord Rees to point out that our own planet suits us well and is extraordinarily congenial on climate, landscape and oxygen so why not leave it to robots to explore the universe while we get on with saving planet earth.

Who wants to live on Mars or to live eternally in hybrid form, half human half robot? The meaning I seek is from humankind's harmony with the universe and the expression of it is Bach.

The composer Errollyn Wallen knows where meaning lies.

She writes: "An early evening drive from Thurso to Strathy listening to the Choir of King's College, Cambridge tells me that another year is coming to an end. There is a particular point, just after crossing the border from Caithness to Sutherland, where the landscape suddenly opens up wide and becomes wilder. The sky is enormous. The clouds roll across the mountains in the gloaming and the dark calls out to the deer and small creatures huddled in hole. I drive through Reay, Melvich, then straight onto Strathy Point."

It is what Brahms, Beethoven, and Bach knew was the greatest mystery of all.

Constellations and consolation. I think what Kit, the bohemian cabaret star, became at the very end of his life was a pilgrim. He had lost everything of material value but embraced the idea of making paths between churches in Norfolk and restoring nature to the cathedral lake. I think I see the shape of him on the opposite path, tending his mouldy old rowing boat, with those artistic hands. His head full of music and ideas and jokes.

When I objected to him living alone in the dusty makeshift vestry, he said to me that I had not seen the light pouring through the stained-glass window of the bathroom, the place where he died.

Kit's Walk, created at Highclere Castle, by Kit's faithful friend, Lady Carnarvon